The Book of Saints

by

Mary P. Hallick

Z
FOS
E

Light and Life Publishing Company
Minneapolis, Minnesota
1984

Light and Life Publishing Company
P.O. Box 26421
Minneapolis, Minnesota 55426-0421

ISBN 0-937032-31-X

Good name in man and woman, dear my Lord,
Is the immediate jewel of their souls:
Who steals my purse steals trash; 'tis something nothing;
'Twas mine, 'tis his, and has been slave to thousands;
But he that filches from me my good name
Robs me of that which not enriches him
And makes me poor indeed.

Shakespeare, **Othello**, III iii, 156.

Table of Contents

Prologue

This book had its inception eons ago when, as a little girl, my mother pointed out that my father's name was not correctly translated. What a shock! TOM in English was not ATHANASIOS in Greek. Since that moment, names--their history and meanings--have fascinated me.

Greek names are so meaningful and so beautiful that it is almost sacreligious not to properly translate the names. In most instances, the English equivalent is evident, and if the English counterpart is not immediately apparent, a bit of research at a library will help discover the proper translation. However, when all fails and the English equivalent of the name doesn't seem to exist, then it is appropriate and acceptable to use the name in the original Greek. There is nothing wrong with this. Use your Greek name and use it with pridé!

The time has passed, fortunately, when every foreign sounding name HAD to be Anglecized. When our parents and grandparents immigrated to this country the politcal and social climate was very different than that of today. In the first half of the 20th century, sociologists called America "The Great Melting Pot" and tried to force all ethnic groups into one great "homogenized" society. That did not happen. Those sociologists were wrong. America is a pluralistic society. People are seeking their ethnic identities and are saying, "I'm somebody, too." It is no longer a social stigma to have a foreign name. In fact, in some instances, it is almost a status symbol to have a different sounding name.

This book began to take form when young parents would pose the following questions to my late husband, Fr. Constantine: "What is this Greek name in English?"; "Is this a Christian name?"; or, "When is my name-day?" I was called upon, often, to search for the proper translation and a name file came into existence.

One can ascertain the date of a feast day by checking with the priest, who, in turn, refers to the **Menaion.** Unfortunately, it appears that not all names of saints are listed in the **Menaion** used in America, as it seems that only abridged editions are used here. Therefore, one would need to use the **Menaion** that are in monasteries in Greece. Those names that do not have a listed feast day commerorate the holiday on All Saints Day. (This date is a moveable one which is contingent upon the date Easter is celebrated.)

Finally, it was with the encouragement of our daughters, Athanasia (Thana) and Constance, that all the information in those boxes of cards was put into narrative form. This book would not have, or could not have, been possible if it wasn't for my family--my mother, Sophie Paloumpis, my late husband, Protopresbyteros Constantine Hallick, and our daughters, Connie and Thana. Their encouragement and their comments--positive AND negative--made this project realized.

Mary P. Hallick, Ed. D.

A

In Homeric times people and things had two names: the one given them by men and the one given by gods. I wonder what God calls me?
Miquel de Unamured.

AARON
(aŕ.uhn)

(M) The name AARON is of Hebrew origin and possibly means "mountain high," "lofty," or "the enlightened." Historically, AARON is the original high priest of the Hebrew nation and the older brother of Moses and Miram (Exodus 28:1-4; 40:12-13). AARON is commemorated in the Eastern Orthodox Church[1] on the Sunday of Our Lord's Progenitors, which is the Sunday before Christmas.

ABDIAS
(ab.dī.as)

(M) See OBADIAH

ABIGAIL
(ab.ih.gāl)

(F) The Hebrew translation is "father of joy." ABIGAIL of the Old Testament is the wife of Nabal and later of David (I Samuel 25).

Diminutive forms include Abbe, Abbey, Abbie, Abby, and Gail.

ABRAHAM
(ā.brah.ham)

(M) In Hebrew, ABRAHAM expresses the meaning of "father of a multitude," "exalted father." We read in Genesis 12 that ABRAHAM is the first patriarch of the Hebrew people and the father of Isaac. The Orthodox Church memoralizes ABRAHAM on the Sunday of Our Lord's Progenitors. In addition to ABRAHAM of the Old Testament, there are several ABRAHAMS of the Christian era who achieved sainthood and are remembered in the Orthodox Church. St. ABRAHAM, the patriarch, is commemorated on October 9, and the feast of St. ABRAHAM The Righteous is kept on March 24.

---

[1] The Holy Catholic Apostolic Church or Eastern Orthodox Church shall be referred to as the Orthodox Church in the remainder of this text.

Some diminutive names for ABRAHAM include Abe and Abie.

ABRAM
(ā́.bram)

(M) See ABRAHAM. ABRAM is the earlier form of ABRAHAM.

ACHILLES
(ah.kil.́ez)

(M) This name is from the Greek which means "swift". The earliest ACHILLES that has come down to us is the hero of Homer's **Illiad** who slew Hector in the Trojan War. The name ACHILLES appears throughout history and there is an ACHILLES who is an early martyr.[1] He is the Roman soldier who deserted the Roman army after his conversion to Christianity. ACHILLES suffered the penalty that he was expected to inflict on others. The feast days for the martyr ACHILLES are soleminized on April 24 and August 20.

ACYLINA
(ah.sil.́uh.nah)

(F) The name is from the Greek "akelos" - "an edible acorn." The name ACYLINA appears in the Orthodox Church calendar on April 7, May 9, and June 13 in memory of those martyrs named ACYLINA. The name appears again on September 27 as a "neomartyr." ST. ACYLINA, the neomartyr." ST. ACYLINA, the neomartyr of Salonika refused to convert to the Moslem faith and was subjected to public beatings and lashings. She steadfastly refused to denounce her faith in Christ and the Turkish magistrate finally released her to return to her home. As she was being carried home, she died on September 27, 1764, as a result of the brutal treatment.

Diminutives of the name are Lina and Kiki.

ADA
(ā́.da)

(F) A variant form of ADAH.

ADAH
(ā́.dah)

(F) The name ADAH has many translations. From the Hebrew it means "adornment; beauty"; in Latin it is translated as "noble birth"; where as it signifies "happy" in German. ADAH is one of the oldest of all names known to us, except for Eve, and is the first female name (after Eve) mentioned in Genesis 4:19.

Addie and Addy are diminutive forms of the name.

[1] The Greek word martyr connotes "a witness who testifies to a fact of which he has knowledge from personal experience." The term has come to be excusively applied to those who died for their faith.

ADAM
(ad.'uhm)

(M) ADAM is the progenitor of mankind and is the name of the first man in the Bible, Genesis 2:7; 5:1-5. This name from the Hebrew signifies "from the red earth." The Orthodox Church commemorates the feast day of the first ADAM on the Sunday of Our Lord's Progenitors. A Christian ADAM, ADAM The Righteous, is remembered on January 14.

Diminutive forms are Ad and Addy.

ADDIS
(a.'dis)

(M) A variant form of ADAM

ADONIS
(ah.don.'is) or
(ah.dō.'nis)

(M) ADONIS, of Greek mythology, is famous for his great beauty and was the favorite of Aphrodite who bore him a son and daughter.

ADRIAN
(a.'drē.uhn)

(M) This name is from the Latin which means "man of the seacoast" or "of the Adriatic Sea." The word stems from either the Greek "rich" or the Latin (Hadrian) "black". The ancient town of Adria, which gave its name to the Adriatic Sea, was famous for its black sand. Historically, ADRIAN is a Roman gens[1] or family name. The feast days of the Christian ADRIAN the martyrs are observed on November 1, and February 3. A neomartyr, St. ADRIAN, is memorialized on April 17.

ADRIANA
(a.drē.an.'ah)

(F) The feminine of ADRIAN.

ADRIENNE
(a.'drē.en)

(F) A variant form of ADRIANA.

AEMELIAN
(ah.mē.'li.uhn)

(M) AEMELIAN is a name of a Roman gens and means "emulating; imitating." The feast day for St. AEMELIAN The Confessor is observed on August 8. The Orthodox Church calendar lists several Sts. AEMELIAN as martyrs whose feasts are kept on December 11, and July 18.

AENEAS
(i.nē.'uhs)

(M) The word AENEAS in Greek means "praise." In ancient Greek legend, AENEAS is a Trojan who fought with great valor in the Trojan War; however, the name appears as a Christian name in the New Testament. AENEAS is the Greek or the Grecian Jew who was healed of palsy by St. Peter (Acts 9:33-34) at Lydda.

---

[1] gens - a group of families of ancient Rome claiming descent from a common ancestor and united by a common name, land, cult, and burial grounds.

AGAMEMNON
(ag.a.mem̃ʹnon)

(M) AGAMEMNON, brother of Menelaus, was the king of Mycenae and Argos and the commander-in-chief of the Greek forces in the Trojan War. When he returned home, victorious from Troy, he was murdered by his wife, Clytemnestra, and her lover, Aegisthus.
Aggie and Memnon are diminutive forms.

AGAPE
(a.gaʹpā)

(F) "Brotherly love" is the Greek meaning of this name. Several saints with the name AGAPE and its variants AGAPIOS, AGAPETON, are remembered by the Orthodox Church. AGAPIOS, the martyr among priests, is remembered on January 24; AGAPIOS of Mt. Athos is remembered on March 1; and AGAPE, the martyr, is observed on September 17, and April 16.

AGAPETUS
(ah.gapʹeh.tus)

(M) The feast day for AGAPETUS, the pope and strong defender of Orthodoxy, is celebrated on April 17.

AGATHA
(agʹah.thah)

(F) AGATHA is derived from the Greek which means "good; noble, kind;" "a good woman." The Christian martyr AGATHA was tortured and murdered at Catania, Sicily, possibly during the Decian[1] persecution. Her feast day is celebrated on February 5.
Ag and Aggie are the diminutive forms.

AGATHON
(agʹah.thuhn)

(M) This is the masculine form of AGATHA. In Greek legend AGATHON is one of the sons of Priam (Iliad XXIV) and, historically, AGATHON, is the Greek tragedian, a friend of Plato. Again, the name appears in Christian history as St. Agathon The Righteous. The feast of St. AGATHON is commemorated on January 8, in the Orthodox Church.

AGATHONICE
(ag.ah.thuh.nē̃ʹsē)

(F) "Noble victory" is the translation of this Greek word. St. AGATHONICE the martyr is remembered on October 13.
Aggie and Agatho are diminutive forms.

AGATHONIKE
(ag.ah.thuh.nē̃ʹkē)

(F) A variant spelling of AGATHONICE. Diminutives include Aggie, Agatho and Nikki.

---

[1] Decius is the Roman emperor (249-251) who persecuted the Christians vigorously. He was killed trying to repel the Goths in Moesia.

AGATHOS (ag.ah.thos)	(M) A variant spelling of AGATHON. The martyr, AGATHOS, is remembered on August 20.
AGLAIA (ah.glá.ah)	(F) Greek mythology gives us AGLAIA as one of the Three Graces. The name means "splendor." A Christian, AGLAIA, is martyr and the feast is observed on December 19. The English equivalent is Gloria.
AGNELLA (ag.ne.lah)	(F) A variant spelling of AGNES. See AGNES.
AGNES (ag.nis)	(F) The name AGNES is derived from the Greek adjective, "agnos", which means "chaste, pure." St. AGNES was possible martyred during the Diocletian[1] persecution (c. 304), at the young age of thirteen, Her feast is observed on January 21. In Spain, the ladies changed AGNES to the, then, fashionable INEZ.
AGNETA (ag.nē.tah)	(F) A variant form of AGNES.
AIDA (a.ē.dah)	(F) A variant form of ADAH.
AILEEN (ā.lēn)	(F) An Irish form of HELEN. See HELEN.
AKILINA (ah.kil.ē.na)	(F) A variant form of ACYLINA.
-akis (á.kēs)	A masculine suffix meaning "small" or "little." When affixed to masculine names such as Christos it becomes Christakis, Basil - Basilakis. The preceding consonant is attached to the suffix and the little boys are called TAKIS, LAKIS.
ALATHEIA (a.lath.ē.ah)	(F) A variant spelling of ALETHEA. See ALETHEA.
ALASTAIR (a.lis.tuhr)	(M) A Scottish form of ALEXANDER. See ALEXANDER.
ALDORA (al.dōr.ah)	(F) This feminine name is from the Greek which means "winged gift." Diminutives include Aldie and Dora.
ALEEDIS (a.lē.duhs)	(M) A variant spelling of ALEYDIS. See ALEYDIS.

[1] Diocletian jointly ruled the empire with Maximian (284-305). The empire prospered and grew but there was severe persecution of the Christians and economic measures turned out badly. Finally, he and Maximian abdicated in 305. Diocletian retired to a splendid castle in Salona.

ALENE
(ā.′lēn)

(F) A variant form of HELEN. See HELEN.

ALESANDRA
(a.le.san.′drah)

(F) Italian form of ALEXANDRA. See ALEXANDRA.

ALETA
(a.lē.′tah)

(F) A variant spelling of ALETHEA.

ALETHA
(a.lē.′thah)

(F) A variant of ALETHEA. Also ALETHEIA and ALETHIA.

ALETHEA
(a.lith.ē.ah)

(F) "Girl to be trusted" is the Greek meaning of this feminine name.
    Diminutives include Ali, Letha, Litha, Lithea, and Thea.

ALEXANDER
(aĺ.ig.zań.duhr)

(M) For centuries kings bore the name ALEX—ANDER. Homer's **Iliad** tells us that Paris, the son of the Trojan Priam, was called ALEXANDER by the shepherds who reared him. History gives us ALEXANDER the Great who conquered the world (c. 320 B.C.), and who is alluded to in Daniel 7:6, 8:4-7. In the New Testament, there are four or five persons with this name:
    1) an early Christian, son of Simon of Cyrene, who carried the Cross (Mark 15:21).
    2) a prominent non-Christian Jew in Jerusalem (Acts 4:5).
    3) an Ephesian Jew (Acts 19:33).
    4) a renegade Christian of Rome (I Timothy 4:14).
    5) a coppersmith and apostate from Christianity (II Timothy 4:14).
The Orthodox Church has many saints and martyrs who bear this name and some of the festivals are as follows: August 30 - patriarch; March 16 - archbishop of Jerusalem; October 22 -martyr among priests; and May 26 (1794), neomartyr.
    The Greek name means "defender of men." and there are many diminutives of this name including Alec, Alick, Alexis, Aleck, Ellick, Sandy, Sander, Sascha, Alex, and Xan.

ALEXANDRA
(aĺ.ig.zan.′drah)

(F) The feminine of ALEXANDER. Great cities, royalty, and many women bear this name. The feast day of ALEXANDRA, the queen, is observed on April 21. The diminutives include Alexia, Allis, Alexis, Alexa, Sandra, and the Russians use Shura, and Sacha.

6

ALEXANDRIA (al.ig.zan.'dre.ah)	(F) See ALEXANDRA. The feast days of St. ALEXANDRIA are observed by the Orthodox Church on March 20, and May 18.
ALEXINE (al.ek.'sen)	(F) A variant form of ALEXANDRA.
ALEXIOS (ah.le.'si.uhs) **ALEXIS** (ah.lek.sis)	(M) ALEXIS means "helper" in Greek. There are several saints and martyrs who bear this name but the most famous is St. ALEXIOS, Man of God, whose feast is commenorated on March 17.
ALEYDIS (ah.la.'duhs)	(M) This Greek word expresses "a patient friend." Eddy and Leddy are diminutive forms of the name.
ALFEUS (al.'fa.uhs)	(M) A variant form of ALPHEUS. See ALPHEUS.
ALICE (al.'is)	(F) The meaning of this Greek word is "truth." Diminutives include Alla, Allie, Ally and Kiki.
ALIDIS (ah.lid.'uhs)	(M) A variant form of ALEYDIS.
ALISA (ah.lish.'ah)	(F) A variant of ALICE.
ALISDAIR (a.lis.'dar)	(M) A variant form of ALEXANDER.
ALISIA (ah.lish.'e.ah)	(F) A variant of ALICE.
ALISTAIR (a.lis.'tuhr)	(M) A variant of ALEXANDER.
ALITHA (ah.lith.'ah)	(F) A variant of ALETHA.
ALKMENE (alk.me.'ne)	(F) ALKMENE, of Greek mythology, is Amphitryon's wife, who gave birth to Heracles after being seduced by Zeus. Mene is a diminutive form of the name.
ALLISTER (al.'is.tuhr)	(M) A variant of ALEXANDER.
ALPHAEUS (al.fa.'uhs)	(M) The literal translation of this Hebrew word is "changing." The New Testament mentions two men with this name. They are ALPHAEUS, the father of James (Mark 3:18). The Orthodox Church observes May 26, in memory of ALPHAEUS, the apostle. The diminutives are Alfi, Alfie.

ALPHEUS
(al.fē´uhs)

(M) This Greek name expresses the meaning "god of the river." In the **Aeneid** III, we read that Hercules made use of the waters of the river Alpheus in Elis to help cleanse the Augean stables. However, the name appears in Christian annals and several martyrs of this name are memorialized in the Orthodox Church on November 18, September 28, December 28, and May 10.
Alfi is a diminutive form of the name.

ALTHEA
(al.thē´ah)

(F) "Healthy, wholesome," is the Greek meaning of this name. In Greek mythology, ALTHEA is the mother of Meleager, the hero of the Calydonian hunt.
Thea is a diminutive form.

ALYSA
(ah.lis´ah)

(F) A variant form of ALYSIA.

ALYSIA
(ah.lish´yah)

(F) In Greek, the translation of ALYSIA is "of possessive nature."
Dimunitive forms are Lisa and Lisha.

AMALIA
(a.mal´ē.ah)

(F) A variant form of AMELIA.

AMALTHEA
(am.ahl.thē´ah)

(F) This name is found in Greek mythology and AMALTHEA is the nymph who was the nurse of ZEUS.

AMANDA
(ah.man´da)

(F) "Worthy to be loved" is the meaning of this Latin name.
Mandy is a diminutive form of the name.

AMARYLLAS
(am.ah.ril´uhs)

(F) This Greek word means "fresh; new." AMARYLLAS is a rustic sweetheart, the name of a shepherdess, in the pastorals of Theocritus and Vergil.
Ama, Maryl, and Rillis are among the diminutives

AMBER
(am´buhr)

(F) Variant form of AMBROSINE.

AMBROSANE
(am.brō´sān)

(F) Variant form of AMBROSINE.

AMBROSIA
(am.brō´zhah)

(F) Variant form of AMBROSINE.

AMBROSE
(am´broz)

(M) The literal translation from the Greek is "immortal, divine." St. AMBROSE became Bishop of Milan in 374. He is revered because he, not only converted St. Augustine to Christianity, but, also, defended Orthodoxy. His feast day is celebrated on December 7, in the Orthodox Church.

AMBROSINE
(am.brō.sĭn)

(F) Feminine of AMBROSE. Brosine and Brosy are diminutive forms.

AMELIA
(ah.mĕl.yah)

(F) Many Greek girls are named AMELIA in honor of the first queen of modern day Greece. The Teutonic meaning indicates someone who is "industrious, busy, energetic."

Mellie, Mel, and Millie, are the diminutive forms.

AMOS
(ā.muhs)

(M) AMOS is a prophet of the 8th century B.C. The Hebrew meaning of AMOS is "carried" or "a burden." The Orthodox Church commemorates June 15, as the feast day for Prophet AMOS.

ANANIAS
(an.ah.nī.uhs)

(M) The name ANANIAS is mentioned several times in the New Testament. There is ANANIAS, the husband of Sappria, who was a member of the early Christian church in Jerusalem. When Peter rebuked ANANIAS for lying, he dropped dead (Acts 5:1-6). Further on, in Acts 9:10, we read of another ANANIAS who is a high priest and a member of the Church at Damascus. He restored the sight of Paul after his vision of our Savior. The Orthodox Church commemorates several days in memory for saints named ANANIAS and those days are October 1, December 17, January 26, and March 18.

ANASTASIA
(an.ah.stā.zhah)

(F) ANASTASIA is the feminine form of the Greek ANASTASIOS "of the Resurrection" and the major feast day is Easter Sunday. Early Christian Greeks named their daughters for the beloved Patriarch ANASTASIOS whose feast is commemorated on February 10. Three Christian martyrs of the early Christian Church are remembered by the Orthodox Church. The first ANASTASIA, a virgin, is said to have been a pupil of St. Peter and St. Paul and was slain under Nero (54-60 A.D.). April 15 is observed in her memory. ANASTASIA "the Younger" who was martyred under Diocletian (304) was the wife of Publius, a pagan. Publius gave information against her and, subsequently, she was put to death. Her feast day is observed on December 22. The third ANASTASIA is the Greek maiden who resided in

Constantinople. Justinian (597), sought her as a mistress and, to escape him, she fled to Alexandria where she lived disguised as a monk. March 10, is her feast day.

Diminutives for ANASTASIA are Anna, Stacy, Stacey, Stacie and Anty, also Tasha.

ANASTASIO
(an.ah.sta.́se.o̅)

(M) A variant form of ANASTASIOS.

ANASTAIOS
(an.ah.sta.̄́shuhs)

(M) This very popular Greek masculine name means "one who shall rise again" or "of the Resurrection." Since the name refers to the Holy Resurrection of Our Lord, the major feast day is Easter Sunday. However, there are several men named ANASTASIOS who died for Christ and whose memory is commemorated in the Orthodox Church. Some of these days are as follows: ANASTASIOS the Patriarch, February 10; ANASTASIOS, the martyr among priests, April 20; ANASTASIOS The Righteous, January 22; and ANASTASIOS the martyr, October 25.

Diminutives include Stas and Stacy.

ANATOL
(an.uh.tol)́

(M) Variant form for ANATOLE.

ANATOLIOS
(an.ah.tol.́e̅.hus)

(M) Variant form for ANATOLE.

ANATOLA
(an.ah.to̅l.́ah)

(F) Feminine form of ANATOLE.

ANATOLE
(an.ah.to̅l)́

(M) The Greek definition for this name is "from the East." There are several martyrs who bear this name, but the most memorable is ANATOLE, Patriarch of Constantinople. As patriarch, he attended the Council of Chalcedon which established Constantinople as the leading bishopric of the East. July 3, is observed in his memory.

A diminutive form is Tolly.

ANDRE
(an.dra̅)́

(M) Variant form of ANDREAS. See ANDREAS.

ANDREA
(an.dra̅.́hu)

(F) Variant form of ANDREANA. See ANDREANA.

ANDREANA
(an.dre̅.́ah.na)

(F) The feminine form of ANDREAS. See ANDREAS. The diminutive form is ANDI.

ANDREAS
(an.dra̅.́uhs)

(M) St. ANDREAS, the First called Apostle, is the brother of Simon called Peter (Matthew 4:18; Mark 1:16). St. ANDREAS preached in Asia

Minor, Greece, areas of the Black Sea, and at Byzantium (later named Constantinople). He ordained Stachys, the first bishop of Byzantium (Constantiinople). St. ANDREAS suffered martyrdom at Patras, Greece, where he was crucified on an X-shaped cross; hence, that cross is known as St. ANDREAS' cross. The feast of St. ANDREAS is commemorated on November 30. The name ANDREAS in Greek means "strong, manly."

Diminutives are Andy and Drew.

ANDREE
(an.drē.ah)

(F) Variant form of ANDREANA. See ANDREANA.

ANDERS
(an.duhrs)

(M) Variant form of ANDREAS. See ANDREAS.

ANDRIEN
(an.dri.uhn)

(M) Variant form of ANDREAS. See ANDREAS.

ANDRINA
(an.drī.nah)

(F) Variant form of ANDREANA. See ANDREANA.

ANDREW
(an.drōō)

(M) Variant form of ANDREAS. See ANDREAS.

ANDROMACHE
(an.drom.ah.kē)

(F) In Greek mythology, ANDROMACHE is the devoted and faithful wife of Hector. The word means "fighting with men." In the **Menaoin**[1] of the Orthodox Church there is listed an ANDROMACHE who was martyred for Christ's sake. The Orthodox Church observes this feast day on October 12.

The diminutive forms for ANDROMACHE include Andie, Andro, Makē, and Roma.

ANDROMADA
(an.drō.mā.dah)

Variant spelling of ANDROMEDA. See ANDROMEDA.

ANDROMEDE
(an.drō.mēd)

Variant spelling of ANDROMEDA. See ANDROMEDA.

ANDROMEDA
(an.drom.uh.dah)

(F) ANDROMEDA, in mythology, is about to be devoured by a serpent because her mother, Queen Cassiopeia, bragged that she was more beautiful than the Sea-god; but, Perseus came to her rescue and saved her. The connotation of this Greek word is "the justice of the Lord."

Andie, Andy, Andra, and Meda comprise the diminutive forms of ANDROMEDA.

[1] Menaoin - a set of books, of which there is one for each month of the year, lists the service for the fixed feasts throughout the year and the feast days of the saints and martyrs.

ANDRONICUS
(an.dron.'uh.kuhs)

(M) This Greek name expresses the meaning of "man conqueror." St. Paul speaks of ANDRONICUS in Romans 16:7. ANDRONICUS is a fellow Jew who became a Christian prior to St. Paul's conversion. The Orthodox Church commemorates May 17, for ANDRONICUS the apostle and March 2, September 6, and October 9, for the martyrs named ADRONICUS.

Andro, Ronnie and Niki are diminutives for the name.

ANDRONIKE
(an.dron.'uh.kē)

(F) Feminine of ANDRONICUS. See ANDRONICUS.

ANGEL
(an.'juhl)

(M) The original word in both Hebrew and Greek means "messenger." The Greek "angelos" is a translation of the Hebrew "malãkh." Generally, in the Bible, the word is applied to a race of intelligent beings, a higher order than man. The Orthodox church canonized neomartyrs with this name and observes the dates of September 1, (1680), December 3, (1813), and October 28, (1824), in their memory.

Angie is a diminutive form of the name.

ANGELA
(an.'juhl.lah)

The result of an attempt to derive a feminine name from ANGEL.

ANGELIA
(an.'juhl. lē.a)

The result of an attempt to derive a feminine name from ANGEL.

ANGELIC
(an.jel.'ik)

The result of an attempt to derive a feminine name from ANGEL.

ANGELICA
(an.jel.'ik.ah)

The result of an attempt to derive a feminine name from ANGEL.

ANGELIKA
(an.je.lē.'kah)

The result of an attempt to derive a feminine name from ANGEL.

ANGELINA
(an.jel.ē.'nah)

The result of an attempt to derive a feminine name from ANGEL.

ANGELINE
(ań.je.līn)

The result of an attempt to derive a feminine name from ANGEL.

ANGELIQUE
(an.je.lēk)

The result of an attempt to derive a feminine name from ANGEL.

ANGELYN
(an.jé.lin)

The result of an attempt to derive a feminine name from ANGEL.

Diminutives include Angie, Angy and Kiki.

ANGELL (an.'jel)	Variant form of ANGEL. See ANGEL.
ANGELO (an.'jel.ō)	Variant form of ANGEL. See ANGEL.
ANN, ANNE (an), (an)	Variant forms of ANNA. See ANNA.
ANNETTA (a.net.ah)	Variant form of ANNA. See ANNA.
ANNETTE (a.net)	Variant form of ANNA. See ANNA.
ANNA (an.'ah)	(F) The name represents the Greek form of the Hebrew Hannah, which means "grace" or "gracious." We read in Luke 2:36, that the mother of the Theotokos is named ANNA and the Orthodox Church solemnizes the dates of July 25, September 9, and December 9, in her honor.
ANNORA (an.nor.'ah)	(F) Variant of HONORA, See HONORA.
ANSTYCE (an.stĩs)	(F) A variant form of ANASTASIA. See ANASTASIA.
ANTHEA, **ANTHIA** (an.thē.'a), (an.thĩ.'ah)	(F) The name denotes "flower like" in Greek. St. ANTHEA is the mother of St. ELEUTHERIOS and the Orthodox Church observes October 12 in her honor. Thea and Thia are diminutives.
ANTHEMOS, **ANTHIMOS** (an.'thē.muhs), (an.'thi.muhs)	(M) As noted in the annals of Church history, several men with this name laid down their lives for Christ and the Orthodox Church observes the following feast days. The feast for St. ANTHEMOS The Righteous is kept on June 7; St. ANTHEMOS the martyr among priests is observed on September 3, and St. ANTHEMOS the martyr is memorialized on October 17.
ANTHONY (an.thuh.nē)	(M) ANTHONY is a Roman gens whose meaning is uncertain and perhaps means "beyond praise, priceless." The Orthodox Church commemorates January 17, in honor of St. ANTHONY the Great (250-356) who is renowned as the patriarch of monastic life. Other saints named ANTHONY are remembered on February 12, August 23, September 23, November 7, December 1, March 1, and July 10. Tony is the diminutive form.

ANTHOS (an.thōs)	(M) The Greek word denotes "a flower" or "a blossom." The feast day for St. ANTHOS The Righteous is observed on December 12.
ANTHOUSA (an.thōō.sah)	(F) St. ANTHOUSA, an abbess at a convent near Constantinople in the 8th century, openly venerated the icons and was put to torture under orders of Emperor Constantine. The empress, however, befriended ANTHOUSA and she lived to a very old age. The feasts of St. ANTHOUSA the Righteous are observed on July 27, and April 12. Diminutives include Anthe and Thousa.
ANTICE (an.tīs)	(F) A variant form of ANASTASIA. See ANASTASIA.
ANTIGONE (an.tig.uh.nē)	(F) Ancient Greek mythology gives us ANTIGONE, the loyal daughter of Oedipus, who slew herself to avoid being buried alive for disobeying an edict of Creon. In the literature of the Orthodox Church there is a St. ANTOGONOS (M) a martyr whose feast day occurs on October 13.
ANTOINETTE (an.twah.net)	(F) French form of ANTONIA. See ANTONIA.
ANTON (an.ton)	Variant of ANTHONY. See ANTHONY.
ANTONI (an.tuh.nē)	Variant of ANTHONY. See ANTHONY.
ANTONIO (an.tō.nē.ō)	Variant of ANTHONY. See ANTHONY.
ANTOINE (an.twan)	Variant of ANTHONY. See ANTHONY.
ANTONY (an.tō.nē)	Variant of ANTHONY. See ANTHONY.
ANTONIA (an.tō.nē.ah)	(F) See ANTHONY. Even though the feast may be observed on January 17, for the outstanding asectic St. ANTHONY the Great, there are several women named ANTONIA who achieved sainthood and are remembered by the Orthodox Church on January 9, March 1, and June 12. The name lends itself to many diminutives such as Netta, Netty, Toinette, and Toni.
ANTONINA (an.tō.nē.nah)	(F) Italian form of ANTONIA. See ANTONIA.

ANTONI
(an.'to.ne)

(F) Italian form of ANTONIA. See ANTONIA.

APELLES
(ah.pel.'ez)

(M) In ancient Greece, APELLES is the very famous painter and contemporary of Alexander the Great. The name reappears in Church history and there is APELLES who was a Christian man in Rome. He was an outstanding orator during the early years of Christianity and was respected by St. Paul. APPELLES served as Bishop of Heracleia and was instrumental in converting many to the Christian faith. The Orthodox Church remembers him on September 10.

A diminutive form of the name is Pele.

APHRODITE
(af.ruh.di.'te)

(F) The name APHRODITE comes to us from Greek mythology. She is one of the twelve Olympians who is the goddess of love and is identifed as Venus in Roman mythology. The word APHRODITE means "born from the sea." The short form of APHRODITE is "Aphro" and is found in the Etruscan as "Apru", (perhaps as the "Month of Venus.") and appears in Latin as "Aprilis", which gives us the word April.

Diminutive forms for APHRODITE include Aphro, and Rodi. Even April may be used as a form of APHRODITE.

APHRODOSIOS
(af.ruh.do.'si.uhs)

(M) St. APHRODOSIOS, a martyr for Christ, is remembered on May 4.

APOLLINARIA
(ah.pol.in.uh.re.'ah)

(F) See APOLLO. St. APOLLINARIA'S feast day is solemnized by the Orthodox Church on January 14.

The names Polly and Lina are among the diminutive forms.

APOLLINARIOS
(ah.pol.in.uh.re.'uhs)

(M) See APOLLO. The Orthodox Church observes July 23, as the feast day of St. APOLLINARIOS, who is a disciple of St. Peter and the first bishop of Ravenna.

APOLLO
(ah.pol.'o)

(M) In Greek mythology, APOLLO is the god of the sun, music, medicine, and poetry. In as much as APOLLO is a major god of the pagan religion, the New Testament reveals that there is a Jew of Alexandria named APOLLO. He was a learned and eloquent man, who, through the ministry of St. John the Forerunner, became a Christian (Acts 18:24-28). He visited Ephesus about A.D. 54, publicly proclaimed his faith, was instructed by

Aquila and Priscilla, and he, then, preached among the Jews. He is last mentioned in the New Testament as he is about to start for Crete. Tradition has it that he became the first bishop of Crete. The Orthodox Church remembers St. APOLLOS, the apostle, on December 8.

APOLLOS
(ah.pol.os)

Variant form of APOLLO. See APOLLO.

APOLLUS
(ah.pol.uhs)

Variant form of APOLLO. See APOLLO.

APOSTLE
(ah.pos.uhl)

(M) The word means "messenger" or "an envoy" in Greek. More precisely it means "one who is commissioned by another to represent him in some way." As Christians, it refers especially to a man sent out by Jesus Christ Himself to preach the Gospel. The Orthodox Church remembers APOSTLE, the neomartyr, on August 16, (1684).

APPHIA
(ap.fe.ah)

(F) APPHIA is probably the wife of Philemon, (Philemon 1:2), who opens his house to the early Christian Church. APPHIA lost her life with her son, husband, and their slave, Onesimus. Her memory is commemorated in the Orthodox Church on November 22.

APRIL
(a.pruhl)

See APHRODITE.

ARAM
(a.ram)

(M) "High" is the meaning of this Hebrew word. ARAM is the name of three men in the Bible: the son of Shem (Genesis 10:22); grandson of Nabor (Genesis 22:21); and an ancestor of Our Lord (Matthew 1:3: Luke 3:33). The Orthodox Church remembers ARAM on the Sunday of Our Lord's Progenitors.

ARCHONTISA
(ar.kon.tes.ah)

Feminine of ARCHONTON. See ARCHONTON.

ARCHONTON
(ar.kon.ten)

The word is translated as "ruler, magistrate." September 3, is reserved in memory of St. ARCHONTON the martyr.

ARETA
(ah.re.tah)

Variant of ARETHA. See ARETHA.

ARETTA
(ah.ret.ah)

Variant of ARETHA. See ARETHA.

ARETTE
(ah.ret)

Variant of ARETHA. See ARETHA.

ARETINA
(ah.ret.in.ah)

Variant of ARETHA. See ARETHA.

ARETHA
(a.re.thah)

(F) Feminine of ARETHAS. The Orthodox Church observes the feast day of ARETHAS (M) the Great Martyr on October 24. The name in Greek signifies "virtuous friend."
Diminutives include Aret and Reta.

ARGERE
(ar.jer.e)

(M) The Orthodox Church observes April 3, (1725), the feast day of the neomartyr ARGERE. The name in Greek means "white metal" i.e. silver.
A diminutive form is Argie.

ARGYRE
(ar.ji.rah)

(F) Feminine of ARGERE. See ARGERE.

ARIADNE
(ar.e.ad.ne)

(F) The early ARIADNE of Greek mythology is the daughter of Minos and it is she who gave Theseus the clew of thread with which to find his way out of the Minotaur's labyrinth. The meaning of the name ARIADNE is "the holy one." Although the name reminds us of the pagan religion of the ancient Greeks, the name ARIADNE appears in the roles of the Christian martyrs. ARIADNE, the Byzantine empress, is remembered on August 22, while St. ARIADNE the martyr is memorialized on September 18. She is the Christian slave of a Phrygian prince and she was flogged for refusing to join in pagan rites to celebrate her master's birthday.
Adne, Addie are diminutive forms.

ARIANNA
(ar.e.an.ah)

(F) Variant form of ARIADNE.

ARIANE
(ar.e.an)

(F) Variant form of ARIADNE.

ARISTARCHUS
(ar.is.tar.kuhs)

(M) "The best prince" is the literal meaning of this Greek name. Even though ancient Greek history has ARISTARCHUS (220?-150 B.C.), who is a critic and a grammarian, Christianity also boasts of an equally important ARISTARCHUS. The Christian ARISTARCHUS is a native of Thessalonika and a fellow laborer with St. Paul (Acts 20:4; 27:2). When ARISTARCHUS life was endangered in the riots at Ephesus (Acts 10:29), he escaped, continued to travel with St. Paul, and was a prisoner with him in Rome (Colossians

4:10). The Orthodox Church observes September 27, as his feast day.

Diminutive forms of this name include Aristie, Aristy, Arch, Archie, and Risty.

ARISTEA
(ah.ris.'te.ah)

Feminine of ARISTON. See ARISTON.

ARISTIDES
(ar.is.ti.'dez)

(M) In ancient Greek history we have ARISTIDES the Athenian statesman (c. 520-c. 468 B.C.), who is surnamed "the Just." However, there is a St. ARISTIDES a famous Greek convert to Christianity, who lived in the 2nd Century A.D.

Diminutives include Aristie, Aristy, Ari, and Risty.

ARISTOBULUS
(ah.ris.tuh.bu.'luhs)

(M) In Greek, the name means "best counselor." ARISTOBULUS is a resident of Rome whose household was saluted by St. Paul in Romans 16:10. He was ordained by St. Andrew as bishop of Brittany and served there for twenty years. The Orthodox Church commemorates his memory on October 31.

Diminutives are Aris, Aristo, and Risty.

ARISTOCLES
(ar.is.tok.'l)

(M) This Greek name means "praise for the best." The Orthodox Church observes the memory ARISTOCLES the martyr on June 23.

Diminutives include Ari, Aristo, Aris, and Risty.

ARISTON
(ah.ris.'tuhn)

(M) February 22, is reserved in the Orthodox Church for the memory of St. ARISTON, bishop.

Diminutives include Ari, Aristo, Aris, and Risty.

ARMOND
(ar.mon)

(M) French variation of HERMAN. See HERMAN.

ARSEN
(ar.suhn)

Variant form of ARSENIUS.

ARSENIO
(ar.suhn.'e.o)

Variant form of ARSENIUS.

ARSENIUS
(ar.sen.'e.os)

(M) ARSENIUS The Great is the highly educated Roman who became an escetic in Egypt at the age of forty. He lived there until his death at the age of 95. This Desert Father is remembered by the Orthodox Church on May 7.

Diminutive of the name is Arsi.

ARTEMA (ar̂.tem.́ah)	(M.F) Variant spelling of ARTEMAS. See ARTEMAS.
ARTAMAS (ar̂.ta.muhs)	(MF̂) Variant spelling of ARTEMAS. See ARTEMAS.
ARTEMAS (ar.́tuh.muhs)	(M/F) ARTEMAS, in Greek mythology, is the virgin goddess of hunt and the moon who is identified with the Roman goddess Diane. Even though we are prone to associate ARTEMAS with the pagan religion of the ancient Greeks, the Orthodox Church honors the male Christian ARTEMAS on October 30. ARTEMAS is the faithful minister who cooperates with St. Paul (Titus 3:12). Arta, Tema, and Tammy are among the diminutives of the name.
ARTEMIS (ar.tem.́uhs)	(M/F) Variant spelling of ARTEMAS. See ARTEMAS.
ARTEMON (ar.tem.́un)	(M/F) Variant spelling of ARTEMAS. See ARTEMAS.
ARTEMISIA (ar.́tuh.mizh.ē.ah)	(F) Feminine of ARTEMIUS. See ARTEMIUS.
ARTEMIUS (ar.́tuh.mus)	(M) ARTEMIUS is a jailer of one of the Roman prisons and, with his wife, Candida, and daughter Paulina, is converted by St. Peter. ARTEMIUS was beheaded, and his wife and daughter were buried alive under a pile of stones. His memory is commemorated in the Orthodox Church on October 20. Art is a diminutive form of the name.
ASA (ā.́sah)	In Hebrew, the word ASA connotes "a healer" or "a physician." ASA of the Old Testament is a king of Judah. ASA is commemorated on the Sunday of Our Lord's Progenitors.
ASPASIA (as.pā.́shah) or (as.pā.́zhah)	(F) During the Golden Age of Greece, ASPASIA is the Greek courtesan. She is the mistress of Pericles and conductor of literary and philosophical salon. The word in Greek means "welcome". In the **Menaion** no saint appears with this name; however, the name is still in use today. The diminutives include Aspe and Aspia.
ASTEROPE (as.tuhr.́uh.pē)	(F) Variant of STEROPE.

ASTRAEA
(HESTERIA)
(ah.stēr.́e.ah)
(hes.teŕ.ē.ah)

(F) ASTRAEA, which stands for "star maiden" in Greek, is the daughter of Zeus and Themis of Greek mythology. She lived on earth and blessed the mortals and when her task was finished she was placed among the stars in the constellation Virgo. In church history St. Asterios (M), the miracle-worker, suffered martyrdom and the Orthodox Church observes August 7, in his memory.
Ristie is a diminutive.

ASTREA
(astrē.́ah)

Variant spelling of ASTRAEA. See ASTRAEA.

ASTRED
(as.tred̄)

Variant spelling of ASTRAEA. See ASTRAEA.

ASTRID
(as.trid̄)

Variant spelling of ASTRAEA. See ASTRAEA.

ATHANASIA
(ath.ah.nā.́shah)

(F) Feminine of ATHANASIOS. Girls named ATHANASIA usually observe January 18, for the feast day of their patron saint, St. ATHANASIOS the Great. However, Church history lists several women named ATHANASIA who are martyrs and the Orthodox Church honors these courageous women on January 18, April 18, and October 9.
A diminutive form is Thana.

ATHANASIOS,
ATHANASIUS
(ath.ah.nā.́zhuhs),
(ath. ah. nā.́shuhs)

(M) This name in Greek means "immortal." St. ATHANASIOS the Great lived 293-373 A.D., and served the church well. He was a participant at the Council of Nicaea in 325 A.D., and was Patriarch of Alexandria. The Orthodox Church venerates St. ATHANASIOS on January 18.
Diminutive forms are Athan, Thanase, Thane, and Thanos.
Many boys named ATHANASIOS have had their name mistranslated to Tom or Thomas. This is an incorrect translation for the name Thomas (Tom) means "a twin."

ATHENA,
ATHENE
(ah.thē.́nah),
(ah.thēn̄)

(F) Many girls are still named for the Greek mythological character who is noted as the goddess of wisdom and arts. There is no listing of a saint bearing this name in the **Menaion.**
Thene may be used as a diminutive form of the name.

ATTICUS
(at.́i.kuhs)

(M) The feast day for ATTICUS patriarch is observed on January 8, and the feast days for the martyrs named ATTICUS are kept on November 2, and August 26.

AUGUSTA
(au.gus.tah)

(F) Feminine of AUGUSTUS.
   Diminutives include Gusta and Tina. The name Sebaste is the equivalent of Augusta. See AUGUSTUS.

AUGUSTIN
(au.gus.tuhn)

A variant form of AUGUSTUS. See AUGUSTUS.

AUGUSTINA
(au.guś.tē.nah)

Variant form of AUGUSTA. See AUGUSTUS.

AUGUSTINE
(au.guh.stē)

(M) The Latin meaning is "belonging to Augustus". St. Augustine is the author of the **Confessions** and bishop of Hippo. The Orthodox Church commemorates his memory on June 15.

AUGUSTUS
(au.gus.tuhs)

(M) The Romans conferred the title AUGUSTUS on the first Roman Emperor Ceasar Julius Octavanius. The Latin word means "venerable; exalted, majestic" and when the title was conferred on the Emperor it denoted sanctity--almost divinity. The Greeks Grecized the title as Sevastos -Sebastos. The masculine form in English is Sebastian and the feminine is Sevaste or Sebaste.

AUREA
(au.rē.ah)

Variant form of AURORA. See AURORA.

AUREL
(au.ruhĺ)

Variant form of AURORA. See AURORA.

AURELIA
(au.rē.lē.ah)

Variant form of AURORA. See AURORA.

AURERLIE
(au.reĺ.lĭ)

Variant form of AURORA. See AURORA.

AURORE
(au.rŏr)

Variant form of AURORA. See AURORA.

AURORA
(au.rŏr.ah)

(F) AURORA is the Latin word for "dawn." The Greek counterpart is Eos "the goddess of dawn." The French and German variant form is AURORE, the Slavic variants are Zora and Zorana, and the Persian form is Roxanne. Church history reveals St. AURORA gave her life for Christ and her feast day is celebrated on July 4.
   The name AURORA may be translated as DAWN and the following diminutives may be used Aura, Aurie, Orel, Oralie, and Oralia.

AUSTIN
(aus.'tuhn)

(M) A variant form of AUGUSTUS. See AUGUSTUS.

AUSTINA
(aus.tē.'nuh)

Variant form of AUGUSTA. See AUGUSTUS.

AUSTINE
(aus.tīn)

Variant form of AUGUSTA. See AUGUSTUS.

AVRAM
(a.vram)

(M) A variant form of ABRHAM. See ABRHAM.

B

BACCHUS
(bak.uhs)

(M) In mythology, BACCHUS, the god of grape growing and of wine, is often identified with Dionysus. Church history indicates a Christian man named BACCHUS suffered martyrdom and the Orthodox Church observes the feast of St. BACCHUS, Great Martyr, on October 7.

A diminutive form of the name is Bach.

BAPTIST
BAPTISTE
(bab.tuhst)
(bap.tēst)

(M) The word BAPTIST means exactly that in Greek--"a baptizer." Many who are named BAPTIST celebrate the feast day on January 7, John the Forerunner and Baptizer; however, St. BAPTIST, the martyr, is remembered by the Orthodox Church on February 10.

BAPTISTA
(bap.tist.ah)

(F) Feminine of BAPTIST. See BAPTIST. BAPTISTA, in Greek, means "baptized in God's name".

BARACHIAS,
BARACHIAN
(bar.ah.kī.ahs)
(bar.ah.ki.ahn)

(M) BARACHIAS is the Greek form of the Hebrew word "blessed of God." The Orthodox Church commemorates the feast day of St. BARACHIAS on March 27. St. BARACHIAS is the Persian, who was martyred during the persecution of Sapor II. Many Christians were imprisoned, and BARACHIAS left the security of his monastery to go to the prisons to bolster the courage of the prisoners. During the trials of the Christian prisoners, BARACHIAS gave answers, under questioning, that were so filled with wisdom, that it was thought better to hold the trials at night away from the crowds.

Diminutives are Barry, Barrie, and Bar.

BARBARA,
BARBRA
(bar.bar.ah)
(bar.brah)

(F) The name BARBARA stems from "barbaros" which means "foreign or strange" in Greek. "Barbaros" is an imitation of "baa baa" or babble that foreigners used in speaking a language

23

which was not understandable to the Greeks.

St. BARBARA is a 3rd century Syrian martyr. When her father discovered that she was a Christian, he reported her to the governor of Nicomedia. When asked to denounce her faith, BARBARA refused and finally, her father, himself, beheaded her. The Orthodox Church observes December 4, the feast day for St. BARBARA.

Diminutive forms include Babs, Babetta, Barbette, Babette, Barbie, and Barbe.

BARNABAS
(bar.'nah.bahs)

(M) In Aramaic, the word means "son of exhortation." St. BARNABAS is the apostle whose name is associated with St. Paul. BARNABAS, a Jew of the tribe of Levi and a native of Cyprus, introduced St. Paul to the Apostles and vouched for the genuineness of Paul's conversion (Acts 9:27). BARNABAS is described as "a good man, full of the Holy Spirit, and of faith" (Acts 11:25). It is reported that he sold his estate, and gave his money to the Apostles. The Orthodox church observes his memory of July 11.

Among the names found in the list of diminutives are Barney, Barne, and Barrie.

BARNABE
(bar.'nāb)

Variant form of BARNABAS. See BARNABAS.

BARNABY
(bar.'nah.bē)

Variant form of BARNABAS. See BARNABAS.

BARRIS
(bar.uhs)

(M) This Greek name means "weighty" or "heavy". St. BARRIS, the martyr, is remembered in the Orthodox church on March. 26.

A diminutive form of the name is Barry.

BARSOS
(bar.'suhs)

(M) The feast day for St. BARSOS the Righteous is observed on February 28.

BARTHOLOMEW
(bar.thol.'uh.myōō)

(M) "Son of the furrors; a plowman" is the literal meaning of this Hebrew name. BARTHOLOMEW is not the saint's given name, but it is derived from his father's name, "Thomai," with "bar" meaning (in Hebrew) "son of". St. BARTHOLOMEW, who is sometimes called Nathaniel, is one of the twelve Apostles (Mark 3:18). The feast day of St. BARTHOLOMEW is observed on June 11.

The diminutives for BARTHOLOMEW include Bat, Bart, Barth, and Barthol.

BARTLETT
(bart.lit)

Variant form of BARTHOLOMEW. See BARTHOLOMEW.

BARTRAN
(bar.trahn)

Variant form of BARTHOLOMEW. See BARTHOLOMEW.

BARTLEY
(bar.tlē)

Variant form of BARTHOLOMEW. See BARTHOLOMEW.

BARUCH
(bar.uhk)

(M) In Hebrew, BARUCH means "blessed". The BARUCH of the Old Testament is of a distinguished family in the tribe of Judah. He is a faithful friend of Jeremiah, and wrote down all that the prophet said. BARUCH is credited for writing the apocrophal book which bears his name. The Orthodox Church observes September 28, in memory of St. BARUCH the Prophet. A St. BARUCH appears in Christian history, and the feast for St. BARUCH the Righteous is kept on October 21.

Diminutives of BARUCH are Barrie and Barry.

BARYS
(bar.is)

A variant spelling of BARRIS. See BARRIS.

BASIL
(baz.uhl) or
(bāz.uhl)

(M) The Greek meaning of BASIL is "kingly; royal." St. BASIL the Great is greatly respected in the Orthodox Church. He was of a great Christian family of the fourth century, and a very talented man. He established and set down the rules for monasticism; formalized the Divine Liturgy; and established hospitals, orphanages, and homes for the aged. His feast day is solemnized on January 1, in the Orthodox Church.

The proper translation of this name is BASIL. Unfortunately, many have erroneously translated the name as William and/or Bill. William is a Teutonic name meaning "conqueror." The Latin form Rex, the Old French form Leroy, or the French form Roy is a more accurate translation of the name since the meaning of these words is "king."

BASILIDES
(bas.uh.lī.duhs)

Variant form of BASIL. See BASIL.

BASILIO
(ba.sil.ē.ō)

Variant form of BASIL. See BASIL.

BASILIKI
(baz.uh.lē.kē)

(F) Feminine of BASIL. The name BASILIKI has followed the footsteps of BASIL, and has suffered mistranslation, also. If the name BASILIKI needs an English equivalent, then it would be more proper and more accurate to translate this name as REGINA, since the name REGINA means "queen, princess, noble woman, lady," in Latin. The mistranslations of BASILIKI, which range from Bessie to Vanessa, are incorrect.

Diminutives are Kiki, Lissa, and Vasso.

BASILISSA
(ba.sil.uh.sa)

A variant form of BASILIKI. See BASILIKI.

BEATRICE
BEATRIX
(bē.uh.tris)
(bē.uh.triks)

(F) This Latin word means "blessed, happy." St. BEATRICE and her two brothers, Simplicus and Faustinus, were martyred under Diocletian.

Diminutives included Bea and Trixie.

BENEDICT
(ben.uh.dict)

(M) This Latin word means "blessed." St. BENEDICT founded the Monestary of St. BENEDICT at Mount Cassino, and is remembered for developing the rules of Western monastics. The Orthodox Church commemorates the Feast of St. BENEDICT on March 14.

The name BENEDICT has taken several forms in many countries and is BENEDITTO in Italy; BENOIT in France, BENITO in Portugal; BENEDICT in Germany, and BENET, BENNET or BENEDIX in England.

Benny and Dixon are among the diminutives of this name.

BENEDICTA
(ben.i.dik.tah)

Feminine forms of BENEDICT. See BENEDICT. BENEDICTA is the English translation of EULOGIA.

Binnie is a diminutive form.

BENEDETTA
(ben.uh.dē.tah)

Variant form of BENEDICTA. See BENEDICTA.

BENETTA
(be.net.ah)
BENITA
(be.net.ah)

Variant forms of BENEDICTA. See BENEDICTA.

BETTINA
(be.tēn.ah)

Variant form of BENEDICTA. See BENEDICTA.

BENJAMIN
(ben.juh.muhn)

(M) In Hebrew, this word means "son of the right hand" (signifying fortunate). BENJAMIN, of the Old Testament, is the youngest son of Jacob and Rachel (Genesis 35:16-18). Rachel named him

"Benoni--son of my sorrow," but Jacob called him "BENJAMIN--son of my right hand." The Orthodox Church commemorates BENJAMIN on the Sunday of Our Lord's Progenitors. However, the name BENJAMIN appears often on the Orthodox Church calendar, and the Orthodox Church observes October 13, March 31, June 10, and July 29, in memory of those martyrs named BENJAMIN who gave their lives for Christ.

Diminutives include Ben, Benjie, Benjy, Benny.

BENSON
(ben.'suhn)

A variant form of BENJAMIN. See BENJAMIN.

BERENICE or BERNICE
(ber.uh.ni.'se)
(ber.'nuhs)

(F) In Greek, this name means "bringing victory." BERENICE is the eldest daughter of king Herod Agrippa I and the sister of younger Aprippa (Acts 25:13, 23; 26:30). She was first married to her uncle Herod, and after his death, to avoid suspicion of incest with her brother, she married Polemon, king of Cilicia. Another BERENICE appears in the annals of church history, and this BERNICE is a holy martyr, who is remembered on July 12, in the Orthodox Church.

Diminutives include Bernie, Berny, and Kike.

BERYL
(ber.'uhl)
BERYLE
(ber.'hu.le)

(M/F) BERYL is Hebrew for "jewel, precious." St. BERYL the Righteous is remembered on March 21, in the Orthodox Church.

Among the diminutive forms are found Berrie, Barri, and Berry.

BIAN
(bi.'ahn)

A variant form of BIANOROS. See BIANOROS.

**BIANOR,
BIANOROS**
(bi.'uhn.or),
(bi.uh.nor.'uhs)

(M) BIANOROS, a martyr, was beheaded because of his love for Christ. The Orthodox Church observes July 10, in his memory.

BION
(bi.'on)

(M) BION is the Alexandrian pastoral poet who lived about 250 B.C. He is best known for his work, **Lament of Adonis.**

**BLAISE,
BLASIEN,
BLASIUS**
(blaz), (bla.'ze.uhn)
(bla.'shuhs)

(M) This name is from the Latin "blaesus" which means "deformed, stuttering." BLASIUS is the physician who became bishop of Sebaste in Armenia, and suffered martyrdom about 316 A.D. The Orthodox Church observes his feast on February 11.

Blase, Blas, and Blaz are among the diminutive forms of the name.

BLANDINA
(blan.'din.ah)

(F) St. BLANDINA is a martyr who suffered in the reign of Marcus Aurelius (A.D. 177). She was a slave, imprisoned with her master, who, too, was a Christian. She was subjected to terrible tortures, but remained steadfast in her faith. For this, the Orthodox Church observes her feast on July 25.

Diminutives of this name are Andi and Dina.

BONIFACE
(bon.'uh.fās)

(M) In Latin, BONIFACE means "a benefactor." St. BONIFACE, a Roman by birth, encouraged St. Augustine to write against Pelagrian heresy. The Orthodox Church celebrates the feast of St. BONIFACE, the martyr, on December 19.

Boni, is a diminutive form.

BORIS
(bōr.'is)

(M) In the Slavic language, BORIS means "a fighter". BORIS I of Bulgaria brought Christianity to the Bulgars and Slavs. He was baptized by Patriarch PHOTIOS in 865 A.D., and took the name of Michael in honor of the Byzantine Emperor Michael. May 21, is the feast day of St. BORIS.

BYRON
(bī.'ruhn)

(M) BYRON is from the French which means "from the cottage" or "the bear." Lord George Gordon Byron, the great phil-Hellene and English poet, died at Missolonghi, serving the cause of Greek Independence. Many Greek boys are named in his honor.

C

This day is call'd the feast of Crispian:
He that outlives this day, and comes safe home.
Will stand a tip-toe when this day is named,
and rouse him at the name Crispian.   Shakespeare, **Henry V**

NOTE: C often appears as K.

CAESAR
(se͂:zuhr)

(M) The name Caesar is probably of Etruscan origin and, originally, was the surname of the Julian family in Rome. Julius Ceasar gave dignity to the name, and it became the title of those in his family who ascended the throne. Nero was the last of the line, but the name Caesar was used as a title of imperial dignity. (Incidently the words kaiser, czar, and tzar are variants of the name.)

Many used the name Caesar as a first name, and many who bore this name gave their lives for Christ. An important person of the Christian era to bear this name is St. CAESAR, brother of St. Gregory the Theologian, and the Orthodox Church commemorates the feast of St. CAESAR on March 9.

CAITLIN
(kāt͛lin)

Irish form of KATHERINE. See KATHERINE.

CAIUS
(kā͛uhs)

(M) CAIUS, is the pope who (283-298 A.D.), decreed that a man must go through the minor orders of deaconate and priesthood before becoming a bishop. CAIUS, also known as GAIUS, died a martyr's death during the persecution of Diocletian. The Orthodox Church commemorates his memory on November 5.

CALANDRA
(kah.lan͛.drah)

This Greek name means "like a lark".
Diminutives are Calan and Cally.

CALENDRA
(kah.len͛.drah)

This Greek name means "like a lark".
Diminutives are Calan and Cally.

CALONDRA
(kah.lon.́drah)

This Greek name means "like a lark".
Diminutives are Calan and Cally.

CALESTA,
CALLISTA,
CALYSTA
(kah.leś.tah),
(kah.liś.tah),
(kah.lēs.́tah)

(F) CALLISTA in Greek means "the most beautiful." In Greek legend, CALLISTA is the nymph loved by Zeus and hated by Hera. She was turned into a bear. For the Christian name see CALLISTUS.

CALIXTUS,
CALLISTUS
(kah.lik.́stuhs)
(kah.lis.́tuhs)

(M) CALLISTUS is the masculine form of CALLISTA, St. CALLISTUS born a slave, served a sentence as a convict, was a champion of forgiveness, and died for his Christian faith.

March 6, November 22, and June 20, are days reserved by the Orthodox Church to memorialize those men named CALLISTUS, who died a martyr's death.

The English have translated the name as CEELICT. Cal is a diminutive form.

CALLINIKI
(kah.lī.́nuh.kē)

(F) In Greek, this name indicates "good victory". St. CALLINIKI is the rich lady of Galatia who aided imprisoned Christians, and, for this reason, she was martyred. The Orthodox Church observes March 22, for the feast of St. CALLINIKI the martyr.

Diminutives include Cally and Niki.

CALLINIKOS
(kah.lī.́nuh.kuhs)

(M) Masculine form of CALLINIKI. St. CALLINIKOS, a native of Asia Minor, suffered martyrdom by being burned to death. The Orthodox Church observes his memory on August 23.

Cal and Nick are diminutive forms of the name.

CALLIOPE,
CALLIOPI
(kah.lī.́uh.pē)
(kah.lī.́uh.pī)

(F) The word means "beautiful voiced". CALLIOPE, of Greek mythology, one of the Nine Muses, is the Muse of Epic Poetry. A Christian CALLIOPE stood fast in her faith and was beheaded. The Orthodox Church observes June 8, in her memory.

Cally and Poppi are popular diminutives for this name.

CALLIOPIS
(kah.lī.́uh.puhs)

(M) Masculine of CALLIOPE. November 10, and April 7, are dates observed as the feast days of the men named CALLIOPIS, who died a martyr's death.

A diminutive form is Cal.

CALLIRRHOE
(kah.ler.'o)

(F) The name CALLIRRHOE appears twice in Greek mythology, first as the mother of Ganymede; and next, as a girl whose sacrifice was required in order to end a plague in Calydon.

Cally in diminutive form of this name.

CANDACE
(kan.'dā.sē) or
(kan.duh.sē) or
(kan.dā.'se)

(F) CANDACE, in ancient times, is the hereditary name or title of the queen of Ethiopia or Nubia. "CANDACE" queen of the Ethiopians" is mentioned in Acts 8:27.

Both the Greek and Latin roots of this word signifies "the fire-white" or "glowing," but the word means "candid or pure."

CANDACE is the feminine form of CANDIDOS, and Candee, Candie, and Candy are diminutive forms.

CANDICE
(kan.'dis)

Variant form of CANDACE. See CANDACE.

CANDACO
(kan.'dā.cō)

Variant form of CANDACE. See CANDACE.

CANDIDA
(kan.'di.dah)

Variant form of CANDACE. See CANDACE.

CANDIDOS
(kan.'di.dō)

(M) The Latin meaning of this name is "dazzling white." (See CANDACE) June 10 and January 21, are observed as the feast days of St. CANDIDOS in the Orthodox Church.

CARITA
(kar.ē.'tah)

(F) Italian form of CHARITY. See CHARITY.

CARTER,
CARTERIOS
(kar.tuhr),
(kar.ter.'ē.uhs)

(M) CARTERIOS, a priest in Cappadocia, suffered under Diocletian and his feast day is solemnized in the Orthodox Church on January 8.

CASSANDRA,
CASSANDRE
(kah.san.'drah)
(kah.san.'drā)

(F) The Greek meaning is "entangling men." The The CASSANDRA of Greek mythology is the daughter of the Trojans, Priam and Hecuba, and she was gifted with the power of prophecy. When she refused the advances of Apollo, he caused it that no one believed her predictions.

Cass, Cassie, Cassy, Sandra, and Sandre are the diminutives.

CASSIANE
(kas.'ē.an)

(F) The Orthodox Church commemorates the memory of St. CASSIANE the Righteous on September 7.

CATALINA (kat.uh.lē.nah)	(F) Spanish form of KATHERINE. See KATHERINE.
CATARINA (kat.uh.rē.nah)	(F) Portugese form of KATHERINE. See KATHERINE.
CATERINE (kat.uhr.ēn)	(F) Italian form of KATHERINE. See KATHERINE.
CATHARINA (kath.uh.rē.nah)	Variant spelling of KATHERINE. Diminutive forms include Caron and Catant.
CATHARINE (kath.uh.rin)	Variant spelling of KATHERINE. Diminutive forms include Caron and Catant.
CATHERYN (kath.er.uhn)	Variant spelling of KATHERINE. Diminutive forms include Caron and Catant.
CATHERINE (kath.rin)	(F) French form of KATHERINE. See KATHERINE.
CATRIONA (kat.rē.ō.nah)	(F) Scottish form of KATHERINE. See KATHERINE.
CECELIA (si.sēl.ya) or (sē.sē.lē.ah)	(F) Feminine form of CECIL. The Orthodox Church observes November 22, in memory of St. CECELIA, who was of noble birth, and became a convert to Christianity with her husband, Valerian, and his brother. All three suffered martyrdom for their faith. Cis, Cissy, Kiki, and Lea are diminutives of this name.
CECIL (sē.suhl)	(M) This name is from a Roman gens, and is being used as a masculine name. The name CECIL is from the Latin "caecus" which means "blind."
CECILE, CECILY (se.sēl), (ses.uh.lē)	Variant forms of CECELIA.
CECYLE (sē.sīl)	Variant form of CECELIA.
CECILLIA (si.sēl.ē.ah)	Variant form of CECELIA.
CICILY (sis.uh.lē)	Variant form of CECELIA.
CELESTE (suh.lest)	(F) The word CELESTE means "heavenly" in Latin. The Greek equivalent is "Ourania" or "Urania."
CELESTINE (si.les.tin) or	(M) "Heavenly" is the Latin translation of this name. The Orthodox Church observes the

(si.les.tĭn)

memory of St. CELESTINE, pope of Rome, on April 8. CELESTINE sent St. CYRIL of Alexandria to investigate Nestorius. Cyril carried out an extensive examination, found Nestorius to be heretic, and excommunicated him. CELESTINE approved the action.

CELICIA
(se.lish.′ah)

(F) The Latin meaning of this word is "heavenly." The Orthodox Church commemorates the memory of St. CELICIA on June 21.

A diminutive form is Celia.

CELSUS
(sel.′suhs)

(M) Historically, CELSUS appears as a Roman medical author of the first century A.D., and the Orthodox Church calendar indicates there is a CELSUS who was a martyr. His feast day is observed on January 8.

CHARA
(ka.′rah)

(F) The English equivalent is Joy.

**CHARALAMBOS,
CHARALAMPIS**
(ka.ra.′lam.buhs)
(ka.ruh.lam.′puhs)

(M) The Greek translations in "shining with joy, happiness."

St. CHARALAMBOS of Asia Minor was a priest of a tiny Christian community, and was noticed by the pagan governor who demanded that CHARLAMBOS denounce Christianity or be punished. He refused, suffered great torture, and died a martyr's death in 192 A.D. The Orthodox Church solemnizes the Feast of St. CHARALAMBOS of February 10.

The name CHARALAMBOS has suffered much through mistranslation. Often, the boy is called Harry (HARI). If the name HARRY is used only as a diminutive form, then it is correct. But, if the name Harry is used as a translation of CHARALAMBOS then, that is incorrect, for the name Harry is from Henry, an old High German name, which means "ruler of the house."

It is also customary, in Greece, to use Bobby as a diminutive form of CHARALAMBOS. And this is correct, only if it is used as a form of the name; but when Robert is substituted for CHARALAMBOS, then that becomes a wrong translation. The name Robert is derived from Old High German and means "bright fame."

A closer English translation of CHARALAMBOS is CLARENCE. The name CLARENCE, which is the masculine of Clara, means "bright, illustrious."

CHARICLEA,
CHARIKLEA
(ka.ris.́lē.ah)
(ka.rik.́lē.ah)

"To cry with joy" is the meaning of this Greek Greek name. In the Greek romance **Theagennes** and **Charicles** by Heliodorus (of Syria in 3rd century A.D.), the story recounts the love adventures of Theogennes, a Thessalian, and CHARICLEA, the daughter of the queen of Ethiopia.

Diminutives include Hari, Chari, and Clea.

CHARILAOS
(ka.rē.́lā.uhs)

(M) "Joy of the people" is the translation of this name. The Orthodox Church commemorates the memory of Charilaos, martyr, on August 29.

CHARIS
(shaŕ.is)

(F) In Greek, CHARIS is "grace" or "favor." CHARIS, the martyr, is memorialized on April 16, on the Orthodox calendar. The English equivalent, Grace, may be used for Charis.

Diminutives include Chari and Charie.

CHARISSA
(ka.ris.́ah)

Variant form of CHARIS. See CHARIS.

CHARISSE
(shah.rēs)́

Variant form of CHARIS. See CHARIS.

CHARITY
(char.́i.tē)

(F) The translation from Greek for the name CHARITY is "benevolence." The Orthodox Church observes October 5, in memory of St. CHARITY.

Diminutive forms include Charry and Cherry.

CHARMAIN,
CHARMAINE
(char.́mē.an) or
(kar.́mē.an),
(char.́mān)

(F) "A little joy" is the meaning of this Greek word. The Orthodox Church observes the memory of St. CHARMAIN the Righteous on August 6.

CHIMENE
(chē.mēn)́

(F) A variant spelling of XIMENA. See XIMENA.

CHLOE
(klō.́ē)

(F) "A green herb or a young shoot" is the literal translation of this Greek word. In mythological literature, CHLOE is the title given to Demeter. The New Testament reveals a woman named Chloe, who probably had business connections in Corinth or Epheseus. St. Paul converted a CHLOE to Christianity in Corinth (I Corinthians 1:11).

CHLOETTE
(klō.́et)

A variant form of CHLOE. See CHLOE.

CHLORAS
(klor.́ahs)

(F) "Pale" is the meaning of this Greek word. In Greek mythology, Chloras is the goddess of the flowers.

Diminutives used for this name are Lori and Loris.

CHLORES,
(klor.́uhs)

Variant form of CHLORAS. See CHLORAS.

CHLORI
(klor.́e)

Variant form of CHLORAS. See CHLORAS.

CHLORIS
(klor.́is)

Variant form of CHLORAS. See CHLORAS.

CHRISTIAN
(kris.́chan)

(M) "Belonging to Christ; a believer in Christ" is the English translation of this word from the Greek. Believers were first called Christians in Antioch (Acts 11:26). Many received the name Christian, and many gave their lives for Christ. The Orthodox Church observes May 24, the feast of St. CHRISTIAN, the martyr. Furthermore, many who are named Christian celebrate their name day on Christmas Day.

Chris and Kit are diminutive forms.

CHRISTIANNA
(kris.te.́an.ah)

Variant form of CHRISTINE. See CHRISTINE.

CHRISTINA
(kris.te.́nah)

Variant form of CHRISTINE. See CHRISTINE.

CHRISTINE
(kris.ten)́

(F) Feminine of CHRISTIAN. Many girls who are named CHRISTINE celebrate their name day on Christmas Day. Nonetheless, the Orthodox Church commemorates the feast of St. CHRISTINE the Great Martyr on July 24. Briefly, CHRISTINE was born c. 200 A.D. of a wealthy family in Tyre, Syria. To protect her from the Christians and their teachings, CHRISTINE'S pagan father condemned her to live in a tower. Nevertheless, CHRISTINE learned of and accepted Christianity, and after the death of her father, she freely gave of her wealth to the poor and sick. Her actions so angered the authorities that they had her arrested. She was tortured and gave her life for Christ on July 24, 234 A.D.

Chrissie, Chris, and Tina are diminutives for the name.

CHRISTODULUS
(kris.tod.́uh.luhs)

(M) "Servant of Christ" is the translation of this name from the Greek. The Orthodox Church commemorates the feast of St. CHRISTODULUS on March 16.

A diminutive of the name is Chris.

CHRISTOPHER
(kris.'tuh.fuhr)

(M) The literal translation from the Greek is "Christ bearer." St. CHRISTOPHER'S pagan name is "Reprobus" (which means "very homely" in Latin), and he lived during the reign of Decius (c. 250 A.D.). Even though Reprobus was a member of the imperial Roman army, he was converted to Christianity, and spoke out against those who were cruel to the Christians. Subsequently, he was arrested by his former comrades; however, he spoke to them of Christ, and his former comrades went with him to Antioch instead of taking him to Rome. At Antioch, not only was Reporbus baptized by Bishop Babylas (who named him Christopher), but many of his former comrades also were baptized. CHRISTOPHER, then, ordered the soldier to arrest him which they reluctantly did, and he was taken to Rome where he was tried and beheaded in 225 A.D. May 9, is the day observed in memory of St. CHRISTOPHER.

Diminutives include Kester, Kit and Chris.

CHRISTOS
(kri.'stōs)

A variant form of CHRISTIAN. See CHRISTIAN.

CHRYSANTHE
(kri.san.'thē.)

(F) Feminine of CHRYSANTHUS. See CHRYSANTHUS.

Diminutives include Chris and Anthe.

CHRYSANTHUS
(kri.san.'thuhs)

(M) In Greek, the word means "golden flower." St. CHRYSANTHUS, an Egyptian, and his wife Daria, a Greek, are distinguished for their zeal and practice of Christianity. This led to their martyrdom. The Orthodox Church memorializes St. CHRYSANTHUS on March 19.

A diminutive for the name is Chris.

CHRYSEIS
(krī.'sē.is)

(F) In mythology, CHRYSEIS is the daughter of Chryses, a priest of Apollo. In the Orthodox Church the name appears as that of a Christian martyr. St. CHRYSEIS' memory is commemorated on January 30.

CIDNEY
(sid.'nē)

A variant spelling of SIDNEY. See SIDNEY.

CLARA

An English equivalent of LAMBRINI. The name

(klar.'ah)	CLARA is from the Latin and means "bright."
CLARENCE (klar.'uhns)	An English equivalent of CHARALAMBOS. See CHARALAMBOS.
CLARICE (klar.'ēs)	Variants of CLARA. See CLARA.
CLARISSA (klar.'i.sah)	Variants of CLARA. See CLARA.
CLAUDE (klaud)	(M) Masculine of CLAUDIA. The Orthodox Church observes October 30, as the feast of St. CLAUDE.
CLAUDETTE (klau.det')	Variant form of CLAUDIA. See CLAUDIA.
CLAUDINE (klau.den')	Variant form of CLAUDIA. See CLAUDIA.
CLAUDIA (klau.'dē.ah)	(F) The archaic meaning of this Latin word is "lame." Historically, CLAUDIA was, probably, a freed woman of the Roman imperial household. In II Timothy 4:21, we read about CLAUDIA and, most likely, she is a convert of St. Paul's. The Orthodox Church recognizes March 20, and May 18, for the feasts for the martyrs named CLAUDIA. CLAUDIE may be used for the diminutive.
CLAUS (klaus)	A German variant form of NICHOLAS. See NICHOLAS.
CLEMENT (klem.'uhnt)	(M) The Latin word means "mild tempered; merciful." A Christian Clement, of Philippi, is mentioned in the New Testament in Philippians 4:3. The Orthodox Church observes September 10, for CLEMENT, the apostle; January 23, for CLEMENT Bishop of Angora; November 22, for CLEMENT Bishop of Bulgaria; and November 24, for CLEMENT Bishop of Rome. The diminutive form is Clem.
CLEMENTIA (klem.'uhn.shah)	Variant form of CLEMENTINE. See CLEMENTINE. TIA is a diminutive form.
CLEMENTINA (klem.uhn.tē.'nah)	Variant form of CLEMENTINE. See CLEMENTINE. TIA is a diminutive form.
CLEMENTINE (klem.uhn.tēn')	(F) Feminine of CLEMENT. See CLEMENT.

CLEO (klē.ō)	(M/F) The name in Greek means "famed." Cleo is the leader of the Athenian people during the Peloponnesian War. The name, originally, was masculine, however, today it is used more frequently as a feminine name.
CLEODAL (klē.ō.dal)	Variant spelling of CLEODELL.
CLEODEL (Klē.ō.del)	Variant spelling of CLEODELL.
CLEODELL (klē.ō.del)	(M) "From a famous place" is the translation of this name from the Greek. Diminutives are Cleo and Dell.
CLEODORA (klē.uh.dō.rah)	(F) In Greek mythology, CLEODORA, a nymph, is the mother of Parnassus. Diminutives are Cleo and Dora.
CLEODOXA (klē.od.uh.ksah)	(F) CLEODOXA, of Greek mythology, is one of the daughters of Amphion and Niobe, who is changed into stone as a punishment for her mother's pride. Cleo is a diminutive form.
CLEOMEDES (klē.om.uh.dēs)	(M) CELOMEDES is a member of "One of the Thirty at Athens."[1] Cleo is a diminutive of the name.
CLEON (klē.on)	(M) CLEON is an Athenian politician, and commander of the Peloponnesian War.
CLEONA (kle.ōnah)	(F) Feminine form of CLEO. See CLEO.
CLEONE (klē.on)	(F) Feminine form of CLEO. See CLEO.
CLEOPATRA (klē.uh.pat.rah)	(F) The literal translation of CLEOPATRA is "from a famous father." From ancient history, we know of the famous CLEOPATRA, who is the Queen of Egypt, wife of Ptolemy XII (who was her brother), and the mistress of Julius Caesar and Mark Anthony. Christianity has a CLEOPATRA, known as St. CLEOPATRA the Righteous, and the Orthodox Church observes her memory on November 19. Cleo and Patra are diminutives.

[1] A body of Athenian aristocrats, headed by Critias and Theramenes, who undertook to administer the affairs of Athens at the close of the Peloponnesian War (404 B.C.). They put their opponents to death and set up a Spartan garrison at the Acropolis. Later Thraybulus led the exiled citizens, defeated the forces of the Thirty, killed Critias, restored democratic government, and was recognized by Sparta.

CLETUS (klē'tuhs)	(M) The name CLETUS is a diminutive from Anacletus, who is a pope of the first century. The name Anacletus means "blameless."
CLITE (klī'tē)	CLITE means "looking towards the sun" in Greek.
CLYTE, CLYTEE (klī'tā), (klī'tē)	Variant spellings of CLITE. See CLITE.
COLIN (kol'uhn)	A form of NICHOLAS. See NICHOLAS.
CONON (ko'non)	(M) St. CONON is a martyr, whose feast is celebrated on June 15, in the Orthodox Church. He is a poor shepherd who was put to death under Decius.
CONSTANCE (kon'stuhns)	(F) Feminine of CONSTANTINE. See CONSTANTINE. Diminutives are Connie, Dena, Tina.
CONSTANTIA (kon.stan'shah)	Variant spellings of CONSTANCE. See CONSTANCE.
CONSTANTINA (kon.stuhn.tēn'ah)	Variant spellings of CONSTANCE. See CONSTANCE.
CONSTANTINE. (koń.stuhn.tēn)	(M) The Latin meaning of this name is "firm; faithful." CONSTANTINE The Great, Equal of the Apostles, is the first Roman emperor to accept Christiantity. CONSTANTINE established Nea Roma, and moved the capital to his city, Constantinople. The Orthodox Church solemnizes his memory on May 21. The name CONSTANTINE, a very popular masculine Greek name, suffered mistranslation when our fathers/grandfathers came to America. The diminutive for CONSTANTINE, in Greek, is "Kostas," and when our fathers or grandfathers gave the name "Kosta" to the immigration officials (which the Anglo-Saxon officials could not or would not understand), the name was interpreted as Gus. Obviously, this is not the English equivalent of the name (see AUGUST, AUGUSTUS). The name CONSTANTINE should be translated as CONSTANTINE, and the correct diminutives are Connie, Costas, Dean, Deno, Dino, Kostas, and Tino.
CORA (kor'ah)	(F) The meaning of this Greek word is "maiden." Diminutives include Corrie, and Corry.

CORINNA
(kor.ē.nah)

(F) This is a variant form of CORA. However, there is a CORINNA, the Greek poetess who lived c. 500 B.C. She was from Tanagra, a town of ancient Boeotia, and only fragments of her verse remain.

CORINNE
(kor.ēn)

Variant form of CORA. See CORA.

CORETTA
(kor.et.ah)

Variant form of CORA. See CORA.

CORETTE
(kor.et)

Variant form of CORA. See CORA.

CORINA, CORENA
(ko.rin.ah)
(kor.rē.nah)

Variant forms of CORA. See CORA.

CORNELIA
(kor.nēl.ya)

(F) Feminine of CORNELIUS. In Roman legend, CORNELIA is a model of Roman motherly virtue. When her husband died, she refused to remarry, and devoted herself to the education of her three children. When other mothers boasted of their jewels and riches, and asked CORNELIA, "Where are your jewels?" she proudly put her arms around her boys and said, "These are the only jewels of which I can boast."

Diminutives include Cori and Nellie.

CORNELIUS
(kor.nēl.yuhs)

(M) The meanings of this name are mixed. If we look at the Latin, the word is interpreted a "horn of the sun" which was a symbol of royalty. If we look at the Greek, the word refers to "the cornel tree." (The so-called "cornel-cherry" is actually the dogwood.)

The CORNELIUS of the New Testament is a centurion of the Roman army stationed at Ceasarea, who is the first Gentile convert under Peter (Acts 10:11). The Orthodox Church commemorates his memory on September 13.

Diminutives of the name are Cornel, Cornell, Neal, and Neil.

COSMAS
(koz.muhs)

(M) St. Cosmas and his twin brother St. Damian are early martyrs, and are referred to as the "Wonder-workers." According to Church history, COSMAS and Damian were physicians and offered their service, freely, to the needy. However, they were martyred during the persecution of Diocletian and the Orthodox Church commemorates their memory on July 1.

40

CRESEYDE (kres.'a.dah)	(F) A variant spelling of CRESIDA. See CRESIDA.
CRESIDA, CRESSIDA (kres.'i.dah), (kres.'i.dah)	(F) This Greek name means "the golden one". CRESIDA, a character in Homer's **Iliad,** is the daughter of the Trojan seer, Calchos. She returns the love of Troilus, but then forsakes him for Diomedes. Famous interpretations of this tale appear in Chaucer's poem "Troilus and Crisede" and in a drama by Shakespeare. Cresa and Cressi are some of the diminutives for this name.
CRISPA, CRISPIA (kris.'pah) (kris.'pē.ah)	(F) Feminine of CRISPEN. See CRISPEN.
CRISPEN (kris.'puhn)	(M) "Having curly hair" is the Latin translation of this name. In Acts 18:8, and in I Corinthians 1:14, CRISPUS is a ruler of the synagogue at Corinth who is converted and baptized by St. Paul. A diminutive form is Chris.
CRISPIN (kris.'pin)	(M) Variant spelling of CRISPEN. See CRISPEN.
CRISPUS (kris.'puhs)	(M) Variant spelling of CRISPEN. See CRISPEN.
CRITO (krē.'to)	(M) CRITO is the intimate friend of Socrates who was with him when he drank the hemlock.
CYBELLE (sib.'uh.lē)	(F) CYBELLE, of classical mythology, is the mother goddess of Phrygia who is associated with the Greek Demeter. A diminutive form os BELLE.
CYNAR (sin.'ar)	Variant spelling of CYNARA. See CYNARA.
CYNARRA (sin.ar.'ah)	Variant spelling of CYNARA. See CYNARA.
CYNERA (sin.'uh.ra)	Variant spelling of CYNARA. See CYNARA.
CYNARA (sin.'ah.ra)	(F) The Greek meaning of CYNARA is "artichoke," and the island of CINARA (ZINARA) is the Aegean Sea is famous for artichokes. From mythology, we have CYNARA the "Daughter of the moon." Diminutives include Cyna, Nora, and Narra.
CYNTHIA (sin.'thē.ah)	(F) Feminine of CYNTHIUS. See CYNTHIUS. Cindy, Cyn, Cynthe are diminutives of this name.

CYNTHIUS
(sin.'the.uhs)

(M) CYNTHIUS, from the Greek, means "of or from Mt. Cynthus" which is located on the island of Delos. In Greek mythology, Mt. CYNTHUS is said to be the birthplace of Artemis (the Latin Diane). Christianity has a CYNTHIUS, who gave his life for Christ, and his feast day is solemnized on November 15, in the Orthodox Church.

Diminutives of this name include Cyn, Cynthie, Cyndy and Cindy. The name has become obsolete as a masculine name.

CYPARISSIA
(sip.uh.ris.'e.ah)

(F) In classical mythology, CYPARISSIA "the cypress-goddess" is the epithet for Athena.

Rissa is a diminutive form.

CYPRIAN
(sip.'re.uhn)

(M) This name means "a man from Cyprus" in Greek. Church history informs us that CYPRIAN, a bishop of Carthage, lived in the 3rd century and died a martyr's death. The Orthodox Church observes the memory of St. CYPRIAN on August 17.

CYRIACE
(sir.e.as.'e)

(F) Variant spelling for KYRIAKE. See KYRIAKE.

CYRIACUS
(sir.e.ak.uhs)

(M) Variant spelling for KYRIAKOS. See KYRIAKOS.

CYRIL
(sir.uhl)

(M) This Greek name means "lordly". In early years of Christianity, the name CYRIL was often bestowed on a male infant born on the Lord's Day, Sunday, and the Latin equivalent is Dominic.

The name CYRIL is borne by several saints of the Orthodox Church. January 18, is reserved for the memory of St. CYRIL, the Egyptian, who was a great writer and teacher, and, subsequently, became Patriarch of Alexandria.

The 9th century produced another CYRIL. St. CYRIL, with St. Methodios, preached Christianity to the Slavs. He invented what is known as the Cyrallic alphabet, and he based it on Greek letters. He did this so that the Slavic people would be able to read the teachings of Christ in their own language. Russia and some of the Balkan countries still use this alphabet. The Orthodox Church commemorates the memory of St. CYRIL on May 11.

CYRUS
(si.'rus)

(M) CYRUS is Persian for "throne". St. CYRUS of Alexandria is the medical missionary who attempted to assist a woman and her daughter as they were being persecuted for being Christians. In his endeavor to help them he, too, was martyred with them. The Orthodox Church memorializes his feast day on January 31.

D

"A good name is rather to be chosen than great riches." Proverbs 22:1

DAMALAS
(dam.ah.las)

(F) Variant of DAMALIS.

DAMALES
(dam.uh.les)

(F) Variant of DAMALIS.

DAMALI
(dam.uh.lē)

Variant of DAMALIS.

DAMALUS
(dam.uh.lus)

(F) Variant of DAMALIS.

DAMALIS
(dam.uh.lis)

(F) The Greek meaning of DAMALIS is "a heifer."

DAMARA,
DAMARRA
(dam.uh.rah),
(da.mar.ah)

(F) The literal translation of this Greek word is "gentle as a lamb."
    Mara is a diminutive form of the word.

DAMARIS
(dam.uh.ris)

(F) DAMARIS is the woman of Athens who believed in the message of Paul, (Acts 17:34). She must have been a woman of distinction, and, in all probability, was one of the "Hetairai,[1] which was a highly intellectual class of women who associated with philosophers and statesman. This may be the reason she was in the audience when Paul delivered his address on Mars Hill. The Orthodox Church commemorates the memory of St. DAMARIS of Athens on October 2.

[1] In ancient Greece, this was a special class of women who were courtesans or concubines and were cultivated female companions.

44

DAMASCENE
(dam.'uh.sēn)

(M) "A man from Damascus" is the Greek meaning of this name. St. John of Damascus (700?-754?), is a Greek theologian and Doctor of the Church.[1] The Orthodox Church commemorates his memory on December 4.

DAMIAN
(dā.'mē.uhn)

(M) The translation of DAMIAN, from the Greek, is "tame, domesticated." In legend, the two friends, DAMIAN and Pythias, were so devoted that DAMIAN pledged his life and stayed as a hostage for his friend Pythias. The name DAMIAN appears in Church history and the Orthodox Church observes July 1, in memory of St. DAMIAN the Benevolent, and memorializes St. DAMIAN the Miracle Worker on May 5.

DAMIEN
(da.myan')

(M) Variant form of DAMIAN. See DAMIAN.

DAMON
(dā.'muhn)

(M) Variant form of DAMIAN. See DAMIAN.

DAN
(dan)

(M) The name Dan is from the Hebrew and means "judge." DAN, of the Old Testament, is the son of Jacob and the ancestor of one of the Twelve Tribes of Israel. Samson was a famous Danite.

The Orthodox Church commemorates the memory of DAN on the Sunday of Our Lord's Progenitors.

DANELLA
(dan.el.'ah)

(F) Variant form of DANIELLE. See DANIELLE.

DANETTA
(da.nē.'tah)

(F) Variant forms of DANIELLE. See DANIELLE.

DANIEL
(dan.'yuhl)

(M) From the Hebrew, DANIEL means "God is my judge." In the Old Testament book of DANIEL, DANIEL is the principal character, and it is thought that he is also the author of the book. Even though DANIEL is wise minister to the Babylonian kings, he remains faithful to the Jewish laws. The Orthodox Church observes his memory on December 17.

---

[1] Doctor of the Church - The word doctor comes from the Latin "docere" which means "to teach". In the Old Testament, we read of doctors, i.e. those who explained and interpreted the Law. At the time of Christ, the title was still in use (Luke 2:45).

Under the New Law, Doctors of the Church are those who have received a special gift or charisma (Acts 13:1). St. Paul says, "God indeed set some in the Church, first apostles, secondly prophets, thirdly, teachers (I Corinthians 12:28; Ephesians 4:11). He further describes the role of the Doctor of the Church in II Timothy 4:1-8.

Several men named DANIEL, who laid down their lives or Christ, are memorialized in the Orthodox Church. Some dates are December 11, in memory of St. Daniel the Stylite; February 16, for St. DANIEL the martyr; and St. DANIEL the Righteous on September 12.

Diminutive forms are Dan and Danny.

DANIELLE
(dan.yel)

(F) Feminine form of DANIEL. See DANIEL.

Diminutive forms include Dani and Ella.

DANILO
(dan.uh.lō)

(M) A variant form of DANIEL. See DANIEL.

DAPHNE
(daf.nē)

(F) "The laurel" is the meaning of DAPHNE. In Greek mythology, the nymph DAPHNE is changed into a laurel tree to escape the ardors of Apollo. A Christian DAPHNE is remembered in the Orthodox Church on May 28.

DARIA
(dah.rī.ah)

(F) This is the feminine form of DARIUS, and the name is from the Greek which means "possessing wealth". DARIA, the wife of Chrysanthus, is a martyr, and the Orthodox Church observes the feast of St. DARIA on March 19.

A diminutive spelling is DARI.

DARICE
(dah.rēs)

(F) Variant of DARIA. See DARIA.

DAVENE
(da.vēn)

(F) Feminine form of DAVID, See DAVID.

DAVID
(dā.vid)

(M) The Hebrew translation of this name is "beloved." DAVID, of the Old Testament (1000? B.C.), is the great warrior, author of many Psalms, builder an empire for his son Solomon, and founder of a famous line of kings. This line ruled the kingdom of Judah for more than 400 years until Jerusalem was destroyed in 587 B.C.

The Orthodox Church commemorates the feast of DAVID on December 26; however, there appears, in Church history, several men named DAVID, who were martyred for Christ's sake and the days in their memory are observed on April 13, February 1, and June 26.

Diminutives include Dave and Davy.

DAVIDA,
(dah.vē.dah)
DAVINA
(dah.vīnah)

(F) Feminine forms of DAVID. See DAVID.

Vida is a diminutive form.

DAVITA (dah.ve.tah)	(F) Feminine form of DAVID. See DAVID. Vida is a diminutive form.
DAWN (daun)	(F) The English counterpart of AURORA and ROXANNE.
DEANA (de.añ.a)	(F) Variant of the French form of Diana.
DEANNA (de.an.ah)	(F) Variant of the French form of Diana.
DEANNE (de.an)	(F) Variant of the French form of DIANA.
DEBBORA, (deb.bor.ah), DEBRA (deb.rah)	(F) Variant spelling of DEBORAH. See DEBORAH. (F) Variant spelling of DEBORAH. See DEBORAH.
DEBORAH (deb.uhr.ah)	(F) In the Hebrew language, DEBORAH is "a bee." We read in Judges 4:4, that DEBORAH is a prophetess and a judge of Israel who helped the Israelites free themselves from the Canaanites. The Orthodox Church solemnizes the memory of DEBORAH on the Sunday of Our Lord's Progenitors. Diminutives for the name are Deb, Debbie, and Debby.
DELIA (del.yah)	(F) DELIA is Greek for "of or from the island of Delos." This is a feminine name, and is the epithet for Artemis, who was born on the island of Delos.
DELLA (del.ah)	(F) A variant form of DELIA. See Delia.
DELPHA (del.fah)	(F) This name, DELPHA, is Greek for "larkspur."
DELPHINA (del.fe.nah)	(F) Variant form of DELPHA.
DELPHINE (del.fin)	(F) Variant form of DELPHA.
DEMAS (de.muhs)	(M) This name, possibly, is a pet form of the name DEMETRIOS. In the New Testament, Colossians 4:14, and II Timothy 4:10, a DEMAS is a helper of St. Paul in Rome, and is a companion to St. Paul during his first imprisonment at Rome; however, after awhile, DEMAS deserted Paul.
DEMES (de.mes)	(M) The Orthodox Church commemorates the feast of St. DEMES, the martyr, on April 12.

DEMETRA
(dē.mḗ.trah)

(F) In Greek mythology, DEMETRA is the goddess of fruit, crops, and vegetation. See DEMETRIOS.

Diminutive forms are Deme and Kiki.

DEMETRIOS
(dē.mḗ.trē.uhs)

(M) Masculine form of DEMETRA. In the New Testament, III John 12, we read of a disciple, and probably a minister of high repute, who is named DEMETRIOS. However, Holy Tradition relates the martyrdom of St. DEMETRIOS of Thessalonika, who as a soldier of the Roman imperial army, preached Christianity to the soldiers, and hundreds were converted. When the Roman Emperor Maximianus visited Thessalonika, he ordered DEMETRIOS arrested for his activities as a Christian.

While DEMETRIOS was in prison, his friend Nestor visited him daily and told him of the emperor's giant gladiator, Lyaeus. DEMETRIOS told his friend Nestor to challenge Lyaeus, and that the power of Christian prayer would defeat him. Nestor fought and defeated Lyaeus. This event so angered the Emperor that he ordered the immediate death of DEMETRIOS and Nestor. The Orthodox Church solemnizes the feast of St. DEMETRIOS the Great on October 26.

The name DEMETRIOS has suffered mistranslation, and has been translated as James. James is IAKOVOS in Greek. Perhaps, the mistranslation evolved from the Greek pet name "Mimi" to Jimmy, to James. Since there is no English equivalent for DEMETRIOS, then the name or one of its variant forms can be used, but, definitely, not the name James.

Demmy and Mimi are diminutives of this name.

DEMOS
(dḗ.mos)

(M) On April 10, 1763, DEMOS, a neomartyr, gave his life for Christ, and the Orthodox Church observes his memory on the date of his martyrdom, April 10.

DEMOSTHENES
(duh.moś.thuh.nēz)

(M) DEMOSTHENES is the Athenian general who was prominent in the Peloponnesian War.

DEMOS is a diminutive form.

DENIS
(den.́is)

(M) The French form of DIONYSUS. See DIONYSUS.

DENISE
(den.ēś)

(F) The French form of DIONYSIA. See DIONYSIA.

DENNIS, DENYS
(den.'is), (den.'is)

(M) Variant forms of DENIS.

DESPINA
(des.'pe.nah)

(F) A name used in reference to the Theotokos. The English equivalent is MADONNA. See MADONNA.

DIANA
(dī.an.'ah)

(F) In Roman mythology, DIANA is identified with ARTEMIS of Greek mythology. The name is, evidently, related to several words connoting "brightness." See ARTEMIS.
    Di is a diminutive form of DIANA.

DICE, DIKE
(dī.'se), (de.'ka)

(F) DIKE is the goddess of justice, in Greek mythology.

DIDIMUS
(de.'de.muhs)

(M) This name, in Greek, means "a twin." The Orthodox Church observes September 11, February 20, April 5, and May 24, in memory of St. DIDIMUS.

DIEGO
(de.a.'go)

(M) Spanish form for JAMES. See JAMES.

DIFILOS
(duh.fil.'uhs)

(M) "Two friends" is the Greek translation of this name. The feast of St. DIFILOS is observed on August 20.
    A diminutive form is Filo.

DIMITRI
(de.me.'tre)

(M) Variant form of DEMETRIOS. See DEMETRIOS.

DIMITRY
(de.me.'tre)

(M) Variant form of DEMETRIOS. See DEMETRIOS.

DINA
(de.'nuh)

(F) Greek diminutive form for names such as CONSTANDINA, (Constance).

DINAH
(dī.'nah)

(F) The Hebrew translation of DINAH is "judged." In Genesis 30:21, DINAH is the daughter of Jacob by Leah, and is the only daughter of Jacob who is named in the Holy Scriptures.

DINO
(de.'no)

(M) Greek diminutive form for CONSTANDINO. (Constantine).

DIOGENES
(dī-oj.'uh.nez)

(M) In ancient Greek history, DIOGENES (412?-323 B.C.) is a philosopher who belongs to the Cynic School of Philosophy. It is told that he went through the streets carrying a lantern and said he was looking for an honest man. Christian Church history reveals that a Christian DIOGENES was martyred for Christ's sake, and his feast is celebrated on December 5.
    A diminutive form is Gene.

DIOMEDES
(dī.uh.mḗ.dēz)

(M) In Greek mythology, DIOMEDES is one of bravest chieftains in the Trojan War, next to Achilles, who is the mightiest hero among the Greeks.

The Orthodox Church observes July 3, the feast day of the Christian DIOMEDES, the martyr. DIOMEDES, a native of Tarsus, and a physician by profession, zealously propagated the Christian faith and was martyred under Diocletian.

Incidently, the two islands in the center of the Bering Strait, which separate America and Russia, are named Little Diomede (U.S.A.) and Big Diomede (U.S.S.R.).

Diminutives include Dio, Dimi, and Mimi.

DIONE
(dī.ṓ.nē)

(F) The Greek meaning of DIONE is "the daughter of heaven and earth." DIONE is the female Titan, mother of Aphrodite.

The Orthodox Church celebrates March 8, in memory of the Christian DIONE, the martyr.

DIONYSIA
(dī.uh.nish.ḗ.ah) or
(dī.uh.niś.ḗ.ah)

(F) Originally, the name referred to festivals in Athens in honor of the pagan god DIONYSUS. However, the name is the feminine form of DIONYSUS. See DIONYSUS.

Diminutives are Denny and Dennie.

DIONYSIUS
(dī.uh.nish.ḗ.uhs) or
(dī.uh.nī.sē.uhs)

(M) In Greek mythology, DIONYSIUS, one of the twelve great Olympians, is the god of wine and revelry.

Several men named DIONYSUS achieved sainthood. St. DIONYSUS, the Areopagite of the first century, was converted by St. Paul at Athens (Acts 17:34). The Orthodox Church observes his memory on October 3. Another St. DIONYSUS, bishop of Corinth, is best remembered as an ecclesiastical writer. He recorded the martrydom of SS. Peter and Paul in Rome. His memory is commemorated on November 29, in the Orthodox Church. A 3rd century DIONYSIUS was martyred in Paris, and the French form of DIONYSUS is DENIS.

DIONYSUS
(dī.uh.nī.suhs)

Variant form of DIONYSIUS. See DIONYSIUS.

DMITRE
(duh.mit.rē)
DMITRY
(duh.mit.rē)

Variant forms of DEMETRIOS. See DEMETRIOS.

DOLORES
(dō.lō.ruhs)

(F) This is a Spanish word which means "sorrow of the Virgin."

DOMINGO
(dō.min.gō)

(M) The Spanish form of DOMINIC. See CYRIL and KERIAKOS.

DOMINIC,
DOMINCK
(dom.uh.nik),
(dom.uh.nik)

(M) DOMINIC is Latin for "special to the Lord." (See CYRIL and KERIAKOS.)

DOMINICA
(dō.min.uh.kah)

(F) Feminine of DOMINIC. (See Keriake.) DOMINICA was born in city of Carthage of wealthy parents. At the age of 21, she traveled to Constantinople where she learned of the "new faith" - Christianity - and was baptized by the Patriarch. She remained in Constantinople and became a nun. Her fame as a woman of faith, and her work in the service of Christ became known to all. She lived to be 100 years old, the title "Righteous" was conferred upon her, and the Orthodox Church observes her memory on January 8.

DOMNA
(dōm.nah)

(F) The Orthodox Church observes November 2, in memory of St. DOMNA.

DOMNINA
(dom.nī.nah)

(F) During the persecution of Diocletian, St. DOMNINA and her two daughters suffered martyrdom in Syria. St. DOMNINA is memorialized in the Orthodox Church on January 5, and March 1.

A diminutive form is Nina.

DOMNINOS
(dom.nī.nuhs)

(M) St. DOMNINOS, a young physician, and St. Sylvanus, a Syrian bishop, were condemned to work in the mines, and suffered martyrdom under Maximian. The feast day of St. DOMNINOS is celebrated on October 1, in the Orthodox Church.

Diminutives are Dom and Nino.

DOMNOS
(dom.nuhs)

(M) The Orthodox Church observes the memory of St. DOMNOS, martyr, on March 9.

DONA, DONNA
(dō.nah), (don.ah)

(F) The name refers to "a gentlewoman" in Italian and Spanish. The name DONNA, which is a diminutive of Madonna, refers to the Theotokos (Blessed Virgin).

DONATA
(don.ah.ta)

(F) Feminine of DONATUS. See DONATUS. DONA is a diminutive form.

DONATUS
(don.ah.tuhs)

(M) The name represents "a gift" in Greek. The Orthodox Church commemorates the feast of St. DONATUS, the fourth century Bishop of Epirus, on April 30.

Diminutives include Doman, Donat, and Dino.

DONELA
(don.el.ah)

Variant form of DONELLA. See DONELLA.

DONELL
(don.el)

Variant form of DONELLA. See DONELLA.

DONELLA
(don.el.ah)

(F) In Latin, the word signifies "a little girl." The feast day of St. DONELLA is observed on December 17, in the Orthodox Church.

Don, Donnie, Nell, and Nella are some of the diminutive forms.

DORCAS
(dor.kuhs)

(F) The literal translation of this name, from the Greek, is "girl of dark eyes." The name DORCAS is the same as the Syriac TABITHA, that is "gazelle."

DORCAS, a Christian disciple (Acts 9:36-39), is the pious and charitable women at Joppa who "made coats and garments" for widows. She was raised from the dead by Peter. The Orthodox Church solemnizes the feast of St. TABITHA on October 25.

The diminutives of the name are Dorca and Dorcy.

DORCEA
(dor.se.ah)

(F) Variant spelling of DORCAS. See DORCAS.

DORCIA
(dor.shah)

(F) Variant spelling of DORCAS. See DORCAS.

DORIAN
(dor.e.uhn)

(M) The name is the masculine form of DORIS. Dorey, Dore, and Dory are diminutive forms of DORIAN.

DORINDA
(dor.in.dah)

(F) In Greek, this name signifies "a bountiful gift." The diminutives are Dori, Dorian, and Inda.

DORIS
(dor.is)

(F) The name DORIS is derived from the DORIANS, who were citizens of ancient Greece. In addition, Greek mythology gives us DORIS, the sea goddess, and the mother of the sea nymphs.

DOROTEYA
(dor.o.te.yah)

(F) Russian form for DOROTHY. See DOROTHEA.

DOROTHEA
(dor.ō.thā.'ah)

(F) DOROTHEA is made of two Greek words "doro = gift and thea = god" and means "gift of god."

Among the diminutive forms are Dora, Dortha, and Dotty. Since the letter "r" is etymologically converted to "l," Dol and Dolly are also included in the diminutive forms for DOROTHEA.

DOROTHEOS
(do.rō.'thā.uhs)

(M) Masculine form of DOROTHEA, Several who are named DOROTHEOS are memorialized in the Orthodox Church. St. DOROTHEOS, the holy martyr, is remembered on November 5, 7, December 28, and June 5, and St. DOROTHEOS the Righteous is honored on October 9, and August 13.

DOROTHY
(dor.'uh.thē)

(F) A variant spelling of DOROTHEA. See DOROTHEA.

DOSEA
(dō.sē.'ah)

(F) The Orthodox Church commemorates the memory of St. DOSEA, the martyr, on August 6.

DOUCAS
(doo.'kahs)

(M) The feast of St. DOUCAS is celebrated on April 24, in the Orthodox Church.

DOULA
((doo.'lah)

(F) The word in Greek means "a slave." The Orthodox Church celebrates the feast of St. DOULA on June 15.

DROSIS
(drō.suhs)

(M) The feast days for St. DROSIS, the martyr, are observed on March 22, and July 28, in the Orthodox Church.

DRUCILLA
(droo.sil.'ah)

A variant spelling of DRUSILLA.

DRUSILLA
(droo.sil.ah)

(F) This is the Latin feminine form of DRUSUS. Historically, Livia DRUSILLIA is the second wife of Augustus and mother of Tiberius, (63 B.C. - 29 A.D.). However, another DRUSILLA is mentioned in Acts 24:24, as the wife of Felix.

Drusie is a diminutive form.

DWIGHT
(dwīt)

(M) This name has an interesting history. Some authorities suggest that it is possibly derived from the diminutive DIOT of the Old English BRAITHWAITE, which comes from the Greek DIONYSUS.

E

For it is not names which give confidence in things, but things which give confidence in names.   CHRYSOSTOM.

EDA
(ē.dah)

A variant form of ADAH. See ADAH.

EDNA
(ed.́nah)

(F) The name EDNA appears in the **Apocrypha** and possibly comes from the Hebrew "EDNAH" which means "rejuvenation." It is also related to the Hebrew EDHEN, EDEN. The Greeks interpreted the word to mean "delight."

EFRAM, EFREM
(ē.́fram), (ē.́frem)

(M) Variant forms of EPHRAIM. See EPHRAIM.

EFROSENE
(e.fros.́uh.nē)

(F) Variant spelling of EPHROSENE. See EPHROSENE.

EILEEN
(ī.lēn)́

(F) Possibly, Irish form of EVELYN, from EIBHILIN, which is the equivalent of HELEN.

EIREEN
(ē.rē.nē)

(F) Norse form of IRENE. See IRENE.

EITIENNE.
(et.yen)́

(M) French form of STEPHEN. See STEPHEN.

EKATERINA
(e.ka.tuh.rē.́nah)

(F) Russian form of KATHERINE. See KATHERINE.

ELAINE
(ē.lān)́

(F) An old French form of HELEN from the Greek HELENE.

ELEANOR,
ELINOR
(el.́uh.nuhr)
el.́i.nuhr)

A form of HELEN used by the English during the Middle Ages. See HELEN.

ELEANORA
(e.le.nor.́ah)

(F) The Italian form of ELEANOR. See ELEANOR.

ELEAZER
(el.ē.a.́zuhr)

(M) The Hebrew meaning of this name is "God has helped." In the Old Testament, the name is mentioned several times; however, the three men named ELEAZER who are of major importance are: (1) the third son of Aaron (Exodus 6:23); (2) the son of Abinadab whose honored task is to care for the Ark (I Samuel 7:1); and (3) one of David's champions (II Samuel 23:9; I Chronicles 11:11-18).

The Orthodox Church observes the feast of St. ELEAZER the Just on September 2.

ELECTRA,
ELEKTRA
(i.lek.trah)
(e.lek.trah)

(F) "Shining bright" is the meaning of this word from the Greek. In Greek mythology, ELECTRA is the daughter of Clytemnestra and Agamemnon. With her brother Orestes, ELECTRA avenged the murder of her father, Agamemnon by killing their mother and her lover, Aegisthus.

ELENA, ELENE
(e.len.ah), (e.len.e)

Modern Greek form of HELENE. See HELEN.

ELESA
(e.lis.ah)

(F) The Orthodox Church observes the feast of St. ELESA the Righteous on August 1.

ELEUTHER
(e.loo.thuhr)

(M) A variant form of ELEUTHERIOS. See ELEUTHERIOS.

ELEUTHERA
(e.loo.theh.rah)

(F) Feminine form of ELEUTHERIOS. See ELEUTHERIOS.

Diminutive forms include Ellie, Terrie, and Terry.

ELEUTHERIOS
(e.loo.the.re.uhs)

(M) The meaning of the Greek name is "freedom; liberty." St. ELEUTHERIOS, the martyr, is commemorated in the Orthodox Church on August 8. He served as chamberlain to Emperor Maximian Galerius in Constantinople. When ELEUTHERIOS became a Christian, he retired to Bithynia, but was soon arrested and, subsequently, beheaded. St. ELEUTHERIOS the Righteous is remembered on December 15.

Terry is a diminutive form of the name.

ELIAS
(i.li.uhs)

(M) The Hebrew translation is "Jehovah is my God," or "the Lord is my God." ELIAS is the renowned prophet whose mission was to challenge, almost singlehanded, the Baal worship which was brought from Tyre by King Ahab (I Kings 17, 19). In II Kings 2:11-13, ELIJAH (the Hebrew form of the word) is taken up in a whirlwind and his death is not mentioned; however, it was believed that he would return. Thus, in John

1:21, we read that some questioned John the Baptist if he were ELIJAH and in Matthew 16:14, others saw him in Jesus.

The Orthodox Church memorializes the Prophet ELIAS on July 20.

ELIAZAR
(el.ē.ā.´zuhr)

(M) A variant spelling of ELEAZER. See ELEAZER.

ELIEZAR
(el.ī.´zuhr)

(M) A variant spelling of ELEAZER. See ELEAZER.

ELI
(ē.lī´)

(M) A diminutive form of ELIAS. See ELIAS.

ELIHU
(el.´uh.hū)

(M) A form of ELIAS. See ELIAS.

ELIOT, ELLIOT
(el.ē.uht), (el.ē.uht)

(M) A form of ELLIS from ELIAS. See ELIAS.

**ELISABETH,
ELIZABETH**
(i.lis.´uh.buhth)
(i.liz.´uh.buhth)

(F) In Hebrew, the name means "consecrated to God". The famous ELIZABETH is the wife of Zacharias, mother of John the Baptist, and a relative of the Theotokos (Luke 1:5-25, 36, 39-80). The Orthodox Church memorializes St. ELIZABETH on September 5. Others named ELIZABETH suffered martyrdom and are remembered on October 22, June 24, and April 24.

Diminutives of the name are many of which some are Bess, Bessie, Betsy, Betty, Liz, Lizzy, Libby, Lisa, Liza, and Lisbet.

ELISHA
(i.lī.´shah)

(M) "The Lord is salvation" is the meaning of this Hebrew name. ELISHA is the pupil and successor of ELIJAH. The Greek form of the name is ELISEUS. (Luke 4:27). The Orthodox Church observes June 14, in memory of the Holy Prophet.

ELIZA
(i.lī.´zah)

(F) This is the sixteenth century English form of ELIZABETH. See ELIZABETH.

ELLEN
(el.´uhn)

(F) An early English form for HELEN. See HELEN.

ELLIS
(el.´is)

(M) The Old French form for ELIAS. See ELIAS.

ELMO
(el.´mō)

(M) The name ELMO arrived through ERMO, the Italian corrupting of ERASMUS. The word means "friendly" in Greek. Light, sometimes seen at mastheads of ships after storms, is called St.

ELMO's Fire (or less correctly, St. Helen's Fire) and is believed to be a sign of protection for sailors. See ERASMUS.

ELPINIKI
(el.pin.uh.kē)

(F) This Greek name means "hopeful Victory." Niki is a diminutive for the name.

ELPIS
(el.puhs)

(F) The English equivalent of HOPE. See HOPE.

ELSIE
(el.sē)

(F) A Scottish shortened form of ELIZABETH. See ELIZABETH.

ELSPETH
(els.peth)

(F) A Scottish form of ELIZABETH. See ELIZABETH.

EMERALD
(em.uhr.uhld)

(MF) A precious stone of fine green color, in ancient times, was found in Ethiopia, but in modern times, it is only found in South America. A reference is made to the EMERALD in Revelations 4:3, and in Exodus 28:18. The ancients believed that an EMERALD protected the chastity of the wearer.

The Orthodox Church commemorates St. Smaragthos (EMERALD) on March 9.

EMIL
(ā.muhl)

(M) EMIL is from the Latin which means "imitating" and is a variant form of AEMILIUS, a name of a Roman gens. See AEMILIUS.

EMILIA
(a.mē.lya)

(F) The feminine form of EMIL. See EMIL.

EMILIE, EMILY
(em.uh.lī), (em.uh.lē)

(F) Variant forms of EMILIA. See EMILIA.

EMMANUEL
(ē.man.ū.el)

(M) "God with us" is the Hebrew translation of this name. EMMANUEL is a Messianic title which is derived from Isaiah 7:14; 8:8, and in Matthew 1:23, it is declared that the name is divinely applied to the Child Jesus.

Many who are blessed to carry this name, observe this name day on Christmas day; however, the memory of St. EMMANUEL is observed on March 20, in the Orthodox Church.

EMMANUELA
(ē.man.ū.el.ah)

(F) Feminine form of EMMANUEL. See EMMANUEL.

ENID
(ē.nid)

(F) This word is from the middle Welsh word "eneit" which means "soul." However, eneit has its roots, in the Greek word anemos = wind.

ENOCH
(ē.nuhk)

(M) The Hebrew meaning of this name is "devoted; consecrated; dedicated." In Genesis 4:17, ENOCH is the eldest son of Cain, and it is in his honor that the first city named in the Bible is called ENOCH. The Orthodox Church memorializes ENOCH on the Sunday of Our Lord's Progenitors.

ENOS
(ē.nuhs)

(M) The literal translation of this Hebrew word is "man." ENOS is the grandson of Adam, son of Seth, and father of CAINAM. ENOS is remembered in the Orthodox Church on the Sunday of Our Lord's Progenitors.

EPAMINONDAS
(e.puh.min.on.duhs)

(M) The great general and statesman of Thebes was born about 418 B.C., and died in the battle of Mantineia at Arcadia, Greece 362 B.C. He was noted for his brilliancy as a tactician.
Nonda is a diminutive form.

EPHRAM,
EPHRAIM
(ē.fruhm)
(ē.frē.uhm)

(M) In Hebrew, EPHRAIM means "double fruitfulness; very fruitful." The Greek equivalent is POLYCARP. EPHRAIM, of the Old Testament, is the second son of Joseph and Asenath (Genesis 41:52). Christian Church history reveals EPHRAIM, the Syrian, who was born in 306 A.D. His father was a pagan priest, but his mother embraced Christianity;, and raised EPHRAIM as a Christian. He was tonsured as a monk and ordained a deacon. He favored monastic life, and became a prolific writer of beautiful hymns in Syrian. Eventually, he became the director of the Syrian theological school, but during the persecution of Christians in 363 A.D., he took refuge at Edessa on the banks of the Euphretes River. His beautiful hymns earned him the appellation of "lyre of the Holy Spirit." The Orthodox Church commemorates his memory on January 28.

EPHREM
(e.frem)

(M) A variant spelling of EPHRAIM. See EPHRAIM.

EPHROSENE,
EPHROSYNE
(ef.rō.sēn)
(ef.rō.sĭn)

(F) This name means "delight, gladness" in Greek. EUPHROSYNE is one of the three Graces of Greek mythology. The name EPHROSENE was taken by Christians, and two women named EPHROSENE achieved sainthood. The Orthodox Church commemorates their memory on September 25, and October 18.
Diminutives are Effie and Affie.

EPICASTE
(ep.e.cas.'tah)

(F) A variant form of JOCASTA. JOCASTA is called EPICASTE by Homer. See JOCASTA.

EPIPHANIA
(e.pif.uh.ni.'ah)

(F) The name is from the Greek word "epiphany"--"manifestation." Epiphany is also called Theophany, which means "God shows Himself to us." Christ was baptized in the River Jordan by John the Baptist, and, for the first time, the Holy Trinity was revealed for all mankind to know and believe. The Feast of Epiphany is celebrated on January 6, in the Orthodox Church.

The English corruption of Theophany is Tiffany.

EPIPHANIUS
(e.pif.an.'e.uhs)

(M) Masculine of EPIPHANY. In Greek, the name is "manifestation of God." The Orthodox Church celebrates January 6, the feast of EPIPHANY. In addition to this major feast in the Orthodox Church, May 12, is reserved for the observance of the feast day of St. EPIPHANIUS. The Palestenian, EPIPHANIUS, is the abbot and ascetic of great repute, who became Bishop of Cyprus in the 5th century. Uncovering heresies was his specialty.

EPISTEME
(e.pis.'tuh.me)

(F) This name is from the Greek which means "knowledge, understanding." The chronicles of Church history indicate that Galation, a Christian, convertred his wife EPISTEME. They, then, each retired to a monestary; however, during the reign of Decius, they were martyred at Emessa in Phoenicia. The Orthodox Church reveres her memory on November 5.

A diminutive form is Teme.

ERASMUS
(i.raz.'muhs)

(M) The name from the Greek means "lovely; worthy of love." The Orthodox Church observes June 2, May 10, and June 18, in memory of the three Christian men named ERASMUS who died for Christ.

ERASTATUS
(i.ras.'ta.tuhs)

(M) Variant spelling of ERASTUS. See ERASTUS.

ERASTES
(i.ras.'tez)

(M) Variant spelling of ERASTUS. See ERASTUS.

ERASTUS
(i.ras.'tuhs)

(M) In Greek, ERASTUS is translated as "beloved; honored son". The name ERASTUS appears in the New Testament, and ERASTUS is a

Christian friend and fellow laborer of Paul. He was a Corinthian and treasurer of the city, but followed Paul to Ephesus. In Acts 19:22, ERASTUS was with Timothy in Macedonia; he was back in Corinth when Paul wrote to the Romans, but remained in Corinth when Paul went as a prisoner to Rome (II Timothy 4:20).

The Orthodox Church observes his memory on November 10.

Eros and Rastus are diminutives.

ERIN
(ē.rin)

A form for IRENE. See IRENE.

ERIPHYLE
(e.rif.uh.lē)

(F) In Greek legend, ERIPHYLE is the wife of Amphiaraus, who was one of "The Seven Against Thebes." She accepted bribes which led to the death of her husband and the murder of her son.

Diminutives include Eri and Fillie.

ERMAS
(ur.mas)

(F) The word in Greek means "ballast." The Orthodox Church observes the feast of St. ERMAS on November 4.

ESDRAS
(es.druhs)

(M) The Greek form of EZRAS. See EZRAS.

ESMERALDA
(es.mer.al.dah)

(F) Greek for "of high value; a jewel." See SMARAGDOS.

ESTABAN
(es.tuh.ban)

(M) Spanish form of STEPHEN. See STEPHEN.

ESTELLE
(e.stel)

The word is from the Latin and means "star."

ESTHER
(es.tuhr)

(F) In Persian, ESTHER means "a star." ESTHER is the Persian name of "Hadassah," who was a daughter of Abihail of the tribe of Benjamin. The Book of ESTHER of the Old Testament recounts the story of ESTHER, a Jewish queen of Persia, who saved her people from massacre. The Orthodox Church memorializes ESTHER on the Sunday of Our Lord's Progenitors.

Among the diminutive names are Ess, Essie, Tess, and Tessie.

ESTUS
(es.tuhs)

(M) A variant form of ERASTUS. See ERASTUS.

ETHAN
(ē.thuhn)

(M) The name ETHAN is translated as "constant" from the Hebrew. The Old Testament reveals two men named ETHAN, and in I Kings 4:31, ETHAN is one of four men renowned for their wisdom. The ETHAN of I Chronicles 6:44, is a Levite, son of Kishi, and one of the three masters of temple music.

EUDOCA
(ū.dō.'kah)

(F) A variant spelling of EUDOCIA. See EDOCIA.

EUDOCIA
(ū.dō.'shah)

(F) This name means "child of a brave father." Church history informs us that EUDOCIA is a beautiful, wealthy Syrian woman who attracted men, even the Emperor, with her charm, wit, and beauty. However, at the age of thirty, she gave up her position and wealth, and became a Christian. She displayed miraculous healing powers, which so displeased the pagan ruler of Syria, that he had her beheaded. The Orthodox Church observes March 4, in her memory.

In addition, the Orthodox Church observes August 13, in memory of Empress EUDOCIA. Her name was originally Athenais. At the death of her father, she was left penniless as he willed all his property to his sons. She traveled to Constantinople to appeal to the emperor for her share of her father's estate. While in Constantinople, she became a Christian and was baptized EUDOCIA. She, subsequently, married the emperor and in 423, was proclaimed "Augusta." Through religious and governmental differences and palace intrigues, she came into disfavor of the emperor, and retired to Jerusalem where she spent the rest of her life.

Diminutives include Docia, Docie, Doxia, and Doxie.

EUDORA
(ū.'dor.ah)

(F) "Generous; wonderful gift" is the meaning of this Greek name.

A diminutive form is Dora.

EUDOSIA
(ū.dō.'si.ah)

(F) A variant form of EUDOCIA. See EUDOCIA.

EUDOXIA
(ū.dok.'se.ah)

(F) A variant form of EUDOCIA. See EUDOCIA.

EUFROSENE
(ū.fors.'uh.nē)

(F) Variant spelling of EPHROSYNE. See EPHROSYNE.

EUGENE
(ū.jēn')

(M) EUGENE means "well born; noble" in Greek. The Orthodox Church honors several men named EUGENE who gave their lives for Christ. These dates are September 25, November 7, 24, December 10, 13, January 21, February 19, March 7, and July 21.

A diminutive form is Gene.

EUGENIA,
EUGENIE
(ū.jē.́nē.ah)
(ū.jē.́nē)

(F) Feminine form of EUGENE. During the reign of the Roman Emperor Commodus (180-192 A.D.), a Roman Perfect was sent to serve in the City of Alexandria. His daughter, EUGENIA, accompanied him there, where she learned of Christianity and subsequently, was converted. She abandoned her household and entered a convent. Eventually, she converted her father, brothers, and sisters to Christianity. Nevertheless, she suffered martyrdom in Rome on December 24, 257 A.D., and the Orthodox Church observes her memory on December 24.

Genie and Ginny are diminutives.

EUHODIA
(ū.ho.́dē.ah)

(F) A variant spelling of EVODIA. See EVODIA.

EULALIA
(ū.́la.lē.ah)

(F) Feminine of EULALIOS. This Greek name means "fair speech; soft spoken woman."

Eula, Lallie, and Ula are diminutives of this name.

EULALIOS
(ū.la.́lē.ahs)

(M) The meaning of this Greek word is "soft spoken man." The Orthodox Church commemorates the memory of St. EULALIOS on August 30.

EULOGIA
(ū.loj.́ē.ah)

(F) Feminine form of EULOGIOS. The English translation is BENEDICTA.

EULOGIOS
(ū.loj.́ē.ahs)

(M) The English translation of EULOGIOS (which means "blessed" in Greek) is BENEDICT. See BENEDICT. The Orthodox Church commemorates the memory of St. EULOGIOS on February 13, March 5, and April 27.

EUNICE
(ū.́nis)

(F) "Happy victory" is the meaning of this name. EUNICE is the mother of Timothy (II Timothy 1:5) and the daughter of Lois. EUNICE was a Jewess, and her husband was a Greek. (Acts 16:1). She transmitted to her son the lessons of truth that she, herself, had received from her pious mother. The Orthodox Church memorializes EUNICE on October 28.

EUODIA (ū.ō.dē.ah)	(M) Variant spelling of EVODIA. See EVODIA.
EUPHEME (ū.fēm)	(F) A variant spelling of EUPHEMIA. See EUPHEMIA.
EUPHEMIA (ū.fem.ē.ah)	(F) In Greek, EUPHEMIA means "pleasant speech," "fairest of the famous." The Orthodox Church commemorates the memory of St. EUPHEMIA the All-extolled Great Martyr on September 16. EUPHEMIA is the devoted Christian woman, who refused to deny God, and was burned at the stake in 303 A.D. Diminutives include Effie, Ephie, Mia, and Phemia.
EUROSYNE (ū.rō.sēn)	Variant spelling for EPHROSYNE. See EPHROSYNE.
EURYDICE (ū.rid.uh.sē)	(F) The Greek translation is "broad separation." In Greek mythology, EURYDICE is the wife of the musician Orestes. When EURYDICE died, Orestes descended to Hades, and so pleased Pluto with his music, that the god allowed him to lead EURYDICE back to earth on the condition that he not look back; but, he did, and EURYDICE vanished into the depths of Hades.
EUSTACE (ū.stas)	(M) A variant spelling of EUSTATHIUS. See EUSTATHIUS.
EUSTACIA (ū.sta.shah)	(F) Feminine of EUSTANTHIUS. See EUSTANTHIUS. Stacy is a diminutive form.
EUSTACIUS (ū.sta.shuhs)	(M) A variant form of EUSTATHIUS. See EUSTATHIUS.
EUSTATHIUS (ū.sta.thē.uhs)	(M) The Greek meaning of this name indicates "healthy, strong." The Orthodox Church observes September 20, in memory of St. EUSTATHIUS, his wife, and two children who suffered martyrdom. In addition, the memory of St. EUSTATHIUS Patriarch of Antioch is commemorated on February 21. Stathy is a diminutive form.
ESTRATIOS (ū.stra.tē.uhs)	(M) "Proper steps" is the literal translation of this name from the Greek. The Orthodox Church observes the memory of St. EUSTRATIOS, the miracle worker, on January 9.

EUTERPE
(ū.tur.'pe)

(F) EUTERPE, of Greek mythology, is the Muse of Music and Lyric Song. The name is translated as "delightful; charming."

A diminutive form is Terpe.

EUTHALIA
(ū.thā.'lyah)

(F) "Growing well; flourishing" is the Greek meaning of EUTHALIA. The Orthodox Church celebrates the feast of St. EUTHALIA on March 2.

Thalia is a diminutive form.

EUTHASIA
(ū.thā.'se.ah)

(F) St. EUTHASIA is remembered in the Orthodox Church on January 12.

Tasia and Tessie are diminutive forms.

EUTHEMIA
(ū.thē.'me.ah)

(F) Femine of EUTHEMIOS. See EUTHEMIOS.

EUTHEMIOS
(ū.thē.'me.uhs)

(M) This name is translated as "to make cheerful." The Orthodox Church commemorates the memory of St. EUTHEMIOS the Great on January 20. St. EUTHEMIOS is the Armenian priest, who at the age of twenty-nine, became a hermit near Jerusalem. Within a few years, he withdrew to a more secluded area near Jerico; however, a community of hermits, gradually, formed about him. His miracles and deeds of charity brought so many Arabs to the faith that the patriarch of Jerusalem ordained him a bishop to care for them. He died at the age of 95, in 473 A.D.

EUTHYMIOS
(ū.thē.'me.ohs)

Variant spelling of EUTHEMIOS. See EUTHEMIOS.

EUTHYMIUS
(ū.thī.'me.uhs)

Variant spelling of EUTHEMIOS. See EUTHEMIOS.

EUTYCHIA
(ū.tik.'e.ah)

(F) Feminine of EUTYCHIOS. See EUTYCHIOS.

EUTYCHIOS
(ū.tik.'e.ohs)

(M) This Greek word signifies "fortunate." EUTYCHIOS of the new Testament (Acts 20:9), certainly, is fortunate, for he is the young man who died when he fell out of a third story window listening to St. Paul preach. His life was miraculously restored.

The Orthodox Church commemorates the memory of several men named EUTYCHIOS who died for Christ. The memory of EUTYCHIOS Patriarch of Constantinople is observed on April 6.

Tyke is a diminutive form of the name.

EVA
(ē.'vah)

(F) This Hebrew name implies "living." EVA is the first mother of mankind (Genesis 2) who was formed from one of the ribs of ADAM. The Orthodox Church commemorates her memory on the Sunday of Our Lord's Progenitors.

EVAN
(e.'vuhn)

(M) Welch form of JOHN. See JOHN.

EVANGELINE
(e.vanj.'uh.līn)

(F) This Greek name expresses the meaning of "bearer of an evangel," or good-tidings," and is related to "angel."

The Orthodox Church observes March 25, the Feast of Annunciation of the Theotokos (Evangelismos).

Diminutives include Angeline, Angel, Angeliki, and Angie.

EVANGELITSA
(e.van.juh.lit.'sah)

(F) A feminine pet form of EVANGELINE. See EVANGELINE.

EVANGELOS
(e.vang.'uh.lohs)

(M) The masculine of EVANGELINE. See EVANGELINE. The Orthodox Church commemorates July 7 for Evangelos, the neomartyr.

Angel, Angie, and Evan are diminutive forms.

EVANIA
(e.van.'ē.ah)

(F) This name means "child of peace" in Greek.

EVANTHE
(e.van.'thē)

(F) The connotation of this name from Greek is "from a flower blossom." The Orthodox Church commemorates the feast of St. Evanthe, martyr, on September 11.

Anthe, Eva and Evie are diminutives.

EVELINA
(ev.uh.lī.'nah)

(F) Variant forms of EVA. See EVA.

EVELINE
(ev.'uh.līn)

(F) Variant forms of EVA. See EVA.

EVELYN
(ev.'uh.lin)

(M/F) The Gaelic form of HELEN IS EIBLIN, and those in the south of Ireland pronounce it as Eileen or Aileen; wherein, those in northern Ireland pronounce it as EVELYN. In the British Isles, EVELYN is used as a masculine name; however, in the United States it is commonly used as a feminine name.

EVODIA
(ev.ō.'dē.ah)

(F) The meaning of this Greek word is "a good journey." In Philippians 4:2-3, we read of two women, EVODIA and SYNTCHE, who perhaps were deaconesses in the Church at Philippi. St.

Paul admonishes them to act harmoniously together in their Christian labors, as all should do who are "in the Lord." The Orthodox Church celebrates the feasts of St. EVODIA on September 1, and September 7.

EZEKIEL
(i.zē´kē.uhl)

(M) This Hebrew name expresses "strength of God." EZEKIEL is one of the four greater prophets and a writer of a book of the Old Testament. The Orthodox Church celebrates his memory on July 23.

A diminutive forms are Zeke and Kiel.

EZRA
(ez´ra)

(M) The Hebrew meaning of this name indicates "help". Ezra is a celebrated priest, and leader of the Jewish nation in the fifth century B.C., and a book of the Old Testament bears his name.

F

A good name is better then precious ointment. Ecclisiastes 7:1

FABIA
(fã.'bē.ah)

(F) Feminine of FABIAN. See FABIAN.

FABIAN
(fã.'bē.ahn)

(M) The Latin translation of FABIAN is "a prosperous ointment." In the 3rd Century B.C., FABIAN is the Roman general who defeated Hannibal by avoiding direct conflict. The Christian FABIAN suffered a martyr's death during the Decian persecution. St. FABIAN preferred martyrdom to hypocracy. The Orthodox Church remembers St. FABIAN, Archbishop of Rome, on August 5.

FAITH
(fãth)

(F) "Trusting, faithful" is the meaning of this Latin name. FAITH, PISTE, is one of the daughters of St. SOPHIA, and the Orthodox Church observes September 17, in her memory. See SOPHIA.

Fay, Fee, and Faye comprise the diminutives of this name.

FAUST
(foust)

(M) This word is translated from the Latin which means "lucky, favorable." In the literature of Goethe and Marlowe, FAUST is the magician and alchemist who sold his soul to the devil in exchange for power and earthly wealth. The Christian men named FAUST were pious men and gave their lives for Christ. The Orthodox Church observes the feast of St. FAUST on September 6, October 4, March 24, April 21, and August 3.

FAUSTA
(foust.'ah)

(F) Feminine of FAUST. February 6, is reserved in the Orthodox Church in memory of St. FAUSTA.

FAUSTINA
(fous.tēn.'ah)

(F) A variant form of FAUSTA. See FAUSTA.

FEBRONIA
(feb.rō.'nē.ah)

(F) FEBRONIA earned the title of St. FEBRONIA Righteous Martyr as she is the young

67

nun who was barbarously mutilated and, finally, put to death under the Diocletian persecution at Nisibis in Mesapotamia. She is remembered in the Orthodox Church on June 25.

Roni is a diminutive form.

FELICE
(fe.lēś)

(F) Variant form of FELICIA. See FELICIA.

FELICITY
(fi.lis.ʹuh.tē)

(F) Variant form of FELICIA. See FELICIA.

FELICIA
(fi.li.ʹshah)

(F) "Happiness" is the meaning of this Latin word and is the feminine form of FELIX. The Orthodox Church observes the feast of St. FELICIA on February 1.

FELIX
(fē.ʹliks)

(M) The meaning of this Latin name is "happy; lucky." The Orthodox Church commemorates the feast of St. FELIX on October 19, April 16, and May 24.

FEODOR
(fē.ʹō.dor)

(M) Russian masculine form OF THEODORE. See THEODORE.

FYODOR
(fī.ʹō.dor)

(M) Russian masculine form of THEODORE. See THEODORE.

FEODORA
(fē.ō.dor.ʹah)

(F) Russian form of THEODORA. See THEODORA.

FEODOSIA
(fē.ō.dosh.ʹah)

(F) Russian form of THEODOSIA. See THEODOSIA.

FEODOSIUS
(fē.ō.dosh.ʹuhs)

(M) Russian form of THEODOSIOS. See THEODOSIOS.

FERN
(furn)

(F) FERN, in Greek, is a delicate plant of feather.

FESTUS
(feś.tuhs)

(M) "Jubilant" is the Latin translation of this word. The feast of St. FESTUS is celebrated on May 24, in the Orthodox Church.

FIDELIA
(fi.dē.ʹlyah)

(F) A variant of FAITH. See FAITH.
A diminutive is Delia.

FILEMON
(fil.ʹuh.mon)

(M) A variant spelling of PHILEMON. See PHILEMON.

FILLANDER
(fil.an.ʹduhr)

(M) Variant spelling of PHILANDER. See PHILANDER.

FILLENDER
(fil.en.ʹduhr)

(M) Variant spelling of PHILANDER. See PHILANDER.

FIRMILIAN
(fur.mil.'uhn)

(M) The Orthodox Church observes the feast of St. FIRMILIAN on October 28.

FIRMIN
(fur.'min)

(M) St FIRMIN, the martyr, is memorialized on June 1, in the Orthodox Church.

FIRMINUS
(fur.min.'uhs)

(M) Variant form of FIRMIN. See FIRMIN.

FIRMON
(fur.'mohn)

(M) Variant form of FIRMIN. See FIRMIN.

FLAVIAN
(flā.'vi.ahn)

(M) This name is from the Latin and means "fair or blonde", St. FLAVIAN served Christ as Patriarch of Constantinople, and the Orthodox Church commemorates his memory on February 16.

FLEUR
(flūr)

(F) Variant form of FLORENCE. See FLORENCE.

FLEURETTE
(flū.'ret)

(F) Variant form of FLORENCE. See FLORENCE.

FLORA
(flor.'ah)

(F) The Romans identified FLORA with the Greek goddess CHLORIS, the goddess of flowers. FLORA is the feminine of FLORIAN.
  Flo and Flossie are diminutives of this name.

FLORENCE
(flor.'uhns)

(F) Feminine form of FLORENTIOS. See FLORENTIOS.
  Diminutives include Flo, Florrie, and Flossie.

FLORENTIOS
(flor.'uhn.tē.ohs)

(M) This name is from the Latin which means "blooming." St. FLORENTIOS, a bishop of Thessalonika during the Apostolic Age, challenged the ruling political powers, who still held to the pagan religion. He preached, not only in the Church, but out on the streets, against those who believed in the pagan gods. He was crucified, and thrown into the fire while still alive. The Orthodox Church commemorates his memory on October 13.
  Flo is a diminutive form.

FLORIA, FLORIS
(flor.'ē.ah), (flor.'uhs)

(F) Variant forms of FLORA. See FLORA.

FLORIAN
(flor.'ē.ahn)

(M) A variant form of FLORUS. See FLORUS.

FLORUS
(flor.'hus)

(M) "Flowering or blooming" is the translation of this Latin name. St. FLORUS and his twin brother, Laurus of Illyria, are the stone masons who handed over a pagan temple (on which they were working) to Christians. As a punishment for their act, they were drowned in a well. The Orthodox Church observes the feast of St. FLORUS on August 18.

FOCAS
(fō.'kahs)

(M) A variant spelling of PHOCAS. See PHOCAS.

FOSTERIOS
(fos.ter.'e.ohs)

(M) The Orthodox Church observes the memory of St. FOSTERIOS on January 5.
A diminutive form of the name is Foster.

FOTINA
(fō.te.'nah)

(F) A variant spelling of PHOTINI. See PHOTINI.

G

Somewhere, what with these clouds,
And all this air,
There must be a rare name, somewhere...
How do you like Cloud-Cuckoo Land?
ARISTOPHANES "The Birds"

GABRIEL
(gā.̃brē.ehl)

(M) The Hebrew translation is "a mighty one of God." GABRIEL is the principal angel or archangel who acts as the messenger of God in the Bible. Three principal angels are named in the Bible--Michael, GABRIEL, and Raphael and only Michael is called an archangel; but, following tradition, the Church gave the title to all three.

GABRIEL is sent to Zacharias to announce the future birth of John the Baptist (Luke 1:11, 19), and he is best known as the Angel sent to give the Theotokos the news of Christ's birth (Luke 1:26-38). The Orthodox Church memorializes Archangel GABRIEL on November 8.

Diminutives of the name include Gabe and Gabby.

GABRIELLA
(gā.brē.el.̃ah)

(F) Feminine form of GABRIEL. See GABRIEL.

Diminutives include Ella, Gabbi, Gabbie and Gabey.

GALINA
(ga.lē.̃nah)

(F) A Russian form for HELEN. See HELEN.

GALINI
(ga.lē.̃nē)

(F) "Calmness; serenity" is the interpretation of this Greek name. St. GALINI is remembered in the Orthodox Church on April 16, for her martyrdom.

GAREFALIA
(gar.uh.fā.̃li.ah)

(F) GAREFALIA is the Greek word for "carnation."

GARMON
(gar.̃mohn)

(M) French form for GERMANUS. See GERMANUS.

71

GASPER (gas'.puhr)	(M) The name of one of the three wise men or kings.
GELASIAS (gel.as'.ē.ahs)	(M) The Latin meaning of "bright star." The martyr, St. GELASIAS, is memorialized on February 27, in the Orthodox Church.
GENNARO (jen.ar'.ō)	(M) A variant form of JANUARIUS.
GEORGE (jorj)	(M) The name GEORGE means "tiller of the soil; husbandman," in Greek. St. GEORGE is the Roman soldier who was martyred at Nicomedia about 303 A.D. He was an officer in the army of Emperor Diocletion, and as a Christian, St. GEORGE refused to make sacrifices to the pagan idols. He gave up his military commission, was persecuted, and, finally, beheaded.

Genevieve January 3 (handwritten annotation)

In the eleventh century, Crusaders found themselves moved by some of the magnificent saints of the Orthodox Church, especially St. GEORGE. They believed that he had come to their aid in a hard fought battle of Antioch, and the Norman Crusaders took him as their patron saint.

The Orthodox Church titles St. GEORGE the Great Saint among Martyrs, the Victory-Clad George, and celebrates his memory on April 23.[1] Others martyrs named GEORGE are remembered on January 8, and February 21.

GEORGETTE (jorj'.et)	(F) French form of GEORGIA. See GEORGIA.
GEORGIA (jorj'.ah)	(F) Feminine of GEORGE. The martyr, St. GEORGIA, is memorialized on August 11, in the Orthodox Church. A diminutive form is Georgie.
GEORGIANA (jorj'.ē.an.ah)	(F) Variant spelling of GEORGIA. See GEORGIA.
GEORGINA (jorj'.ē.nah)	(F) Variant spelling of GEORGIA. See GEORGIA.
GEORGY (jorj'.ē)	(M) Russian form of GEORGE. See GEORGE.
GERIANT (jer'.ē.ahnt)	(M) Variant spelling of GERONTIUS. See GERONTIUS.

[1] If April 23 falls during Great Lent then the Feast of St. GEORGE is celebrated on the Monday following Easter Sunday.

GERASIMOS
(jer.as'.e.mohs)

(M) There are several men named GERASIMOS who served Christ and are remembered in the Orthodox Church. One, who is memorialized, is Abbot GERASIMOS of Palestine. He underwent severe penance, of which, one was to go through all of Holy Lent with no food other than the Holy Eucharist. The Orthodox Church remembers him on March 24. In addition, St. GERASIMOS The Righteous of Cephalonia, who spent his life in search of God, is remembered on October 20. His body has remained in a state of perfect preservation for four hundred years.

A diminutive form of GERASIMOS is Gerry.

GERENT
(jer'.uhnt)

(M) Variant spelling of GERONTIUS. See GERONTIUS.

GEREON
(jer'.euhn)

(M) Variant spelling of GERONTIUS. See GERONTIUS.

GERRON
(jer'.uhn)

(M) Variant spelling of GERONTIUS. See GERONTIUS.

GERMAINE
(jer.man')

(F) Feminine of GERMANUS. See GERMANUS.

GERMAN
(jer'.muhn)

(M) Variant spelling of GERMANUS. See GERMANUS.

GERMIN
(jer'.mihn)

(M) Variant spelling of GERMANUS. See GERMANUS.

GERMANUS
(jer'.man.uhs)

(M) This Teutonic word expresses "bold, outspoken." In 732 A.D. GERMANUS, Patriarch of Constantinople, condemned the "one will heresy" and the beginnings of iconoclasm. Subsequently, Emperor Leo III had him deposed, and twenty years after his death an iconoclast synod condemned him. However, the Seventh Ecumenical Council in Nicaea reversed the condemnation, and praised him for his support of Orthodoxy. The Orthodox Church commemorates his memory on May 12.

GERONIMO
(jer.on'.uh.mo)

(M) Italian for JEROME.

GERONTIUS
(jer.on'.tuhs)

(M) The Orthodox Church remembers the martyr St. GERONTIUS on April 1.

GIACOMO
(ge.uh.ko'.mo)

(M) Italian form for JAMES. See JAMES.

GIANINA (ja.nē'.nah)	(F) Italian feminine form of GIOVANI. See JOANNE.
GIDE (gīd)	(M) French form of GILES. See GILES.
GILES, GILLES (jīls), (gil'.ēs)	(M) The name GILES is a corruption of the Greek word "aegis." Aegis is the shield of Zeus or Athena, and is symbolic of divine protection. St. AEGIOIS is the sixth century Athenian hermit, who went to France to preach. His name was changed from the Greek St. Aegedis to the French form GILLES and GIDE.
GILLIAN (jil.ē.ahn)	(MF) The Anglecized form of JULIANA and/or JULIAN. See JULIANA.
GIOVANNA (jē.ō.van'.ah)	(F) Italian form of JOANNE. See JOANNE.
GIOVANNI (je.ō.van'.ē)	(M) Italian form of JOHN. See JOHN.
GLADYS (glad'.uhs)	(F) The name GLADYS, perhaps, is from the Latin CLAUDIA, the feminine form of CLAUDE. See CLAUDE.
GLAFERA (gla'.fer.ah)	(F) The name GLAFERA is translated as "elegant; graceful," from the Greek. St. GLAFERA is the female slave in the service of Constantia, the wife of the Emperor Licinus. In order to safeguard her chastity, she fled to Pontus to be with St. Basil. She was recaptured and condemned to death, and died on the way to martyrdom. The Orthodox Church commemorates her memory of April 26.
GLIKA (glē'.kah)	(F) A variant form of GLIKERIA. See GLIKERIA.
GLIKERIA (gli.ker'.ē.ah)	(F) "Sweet or sweetish" is the interpretation of this Greek word. GLIKERIA, a Roman maiden, lived with her father in Greece. She was martyred at Heraclea in the Propontis. The Orthodox Church honors St. GLIKERIA on May 13.
GLIKEROS (gli.ker'.ohs)	(M) Masculine of GLIKERIA. The feast of St. GLIKEROS is celebrated in the Orthodox Church on April 24.
GLORIA (glō'.rē.ah)	(F) The English equivalent of AGALAIA. See AGALAIA.

GLYCERIA
(glī.ser.́e.ah)

(F) A variant spelling of GLIKERIA. See GLIKERIA.

GORDIAN
(gord.́e.ahn)

(M) Gordius, an ancient king of Phrygia, tied a knot that, according to prophecy, was to be undone only by the person who was to rule Asia. Alexander The Great cut the knot rather than untie it.

The Christian GORDIAN is the Roman martyr who died c. 250 A.D. The funeral inscription indicates he was a boy. His feast is observed on January 3, in the Orthodox Church.

GRACE
(grās)

(F) The Latin translation is "grace, favor." The literature of Greek mythology tells of the Three Graces who were sister goddesses.--AGLAIA--GLORY, EUPHROSENE--JOY, and THALIA--PLENTY. The Greek equivalent for GRACE is CHARIS. Connected with the word CHARIS is "chairein" "to rejoice," therefore, CHARISSA is derived from the word CHARIS.

The martyr St. CHARIS is remembered by the Orthodox Church on January 28.

GRAYCE
(grā.́se)

(F) A variant spelling of GRACE. See GRACE.

GREGORIA
(gre.gor.́e.ah)

(F) The feminine form of GREGORY. See GREGORY.

A diminutive form is Greer.

GREGORY
(greg.́or.ē)

(M) "Watchful, vigilant" is the literal meaning of this name. Several men named GREGORY worked in the vineyard of Christ, and are remembered in the Orthodox Church; however, the most renowned is St. GREGORY the Theologian, who became one of the four great doctors of the Church. He fought against paganism and heresy; became Patriarch of Constantinople; and he unified the Church into a strong unit so that it could withstand all assaults. The Orthodox Church commemorates his memory on January 25.

GRETA
(grē.́tah)

(F) The German shortened form for MARGARET. See MARGARET.

GRETCHEN
(grech.́uhn)

(F) The German shortened form for MARGARET. See MARGARET.

GRIFFIN
(grif.́uhn)

(M) A variant of the name RUFUS. See RUFUS.

H

*I remember you name perfectly,
but I just can't think of your face.*
W. A. SPOONER

HAIDEE
(hī.dē)

(F) The meaning of this word, from the Greek, is "to caress; respectful, bashful."

HALINA
(ha.lē.nah)

(F) Polish form of HELEN. See HELEN.

HAMON
(ha.mohn)

(M) "Faithful" is the meaning of this Greek name. The Orthodox Church observes the feast of St. HAMON, the martyr, on September 2.

HANNAH
(han.ah)

(F) The meaning of the Hebrew name HANNAH is "grace." In the Old Testament, HANNAH is the mother of Samuel (I Samuel 1-2:21). See ANNA.

HANS
(hanz)

(M) German diminutive form of JOHN. See JOHN.

HARICLEA
(ha.rē.klē.ah)

(F) Variant spelling of CHARIKLEA. See CHARIKLEA.

HARIKLA
(ha.rē.klah)

(F) Variant spelling of CHARIKLEA. See CHARIKLEA.

HARIMON
(har.uh.mohn)

(M) The martyr HARIMON is remembered in the Orthodox Church on August 16.

HARMON
(har.muhn)

(M) French form of HERMAN. See HERMAN.

HECTOR
(hek.tuhr)

(M) HECTOR is the name of the noblest and most illustrious Trojan of the **ILIAD**. Unfortunately, the name has come to mean "to brow beat, to bully".

HELEN
(hel.uhn)

(F) The word HELEN in Greek means "light." Greek mythology gives us the beautiful and famous HELEN of Troy whose face launched a

76

thousand ships. On the other hand, HELEN is the name of the mother of the Emperor Constantine the Great. St. HELEN is closely associated with the discovery of the TRUE CROSS. She is greatly revered in the Orthodox Church, and is memorialized, along with her son St. Constantine, on May 21.

An interesting note in history, is that the Portugese discovered an island in the South Atlantic on May 21, 1502, and named the island in honor of St. HELEN, even though, the Roman Catholic Church observes her day on August 18. The island of St. HELENA was the place of Napoleon's exile from 1815, until he died in 1821.

There are many variants and diminutives of the name as are noted throughout this book. The Gaelic form of HELEN is EIBLIN and those in the south of Ireland pronounce it as EILEEN or AILEEN, whereas those in the northern part pronounce it as EVELYN.

HERACLES
(her.´a.klēz)

(M) In Greek mythology, HERACLES, which means "to the glory of Hera," is the hero of superhuman strength. Orthodox Church literature reveals a St. HERACLES, martyr, who died for Christ, and is remembered on March 9.

Diminutive forms are Herk and Herky.

HERCULES
(hur.´kū.lez)

(M) The Roman variation of HERACLES. See HERACLES.

HERMAN
(hur.´mahn)

(M) The name HERMAN is from the Old German ("hariman-harja = army; mana = man), which means "a noble man." St. HERMAN is the Russian missionary to Alaska, who became one of the first martyrs of the American land. The Orthodox Church commemorates his memory on December 12.

HERMAS
(hur.´muhs)

(M) HERMAS is one of the Apostolic Fathers whose memory is observed on March 8, in the Orthodox Church.

HERMES
(hur.´mēz)

(M) In Greek mythology, HERMES is the messenger of the gods. His Roman counterpart is known as Mercury.

HERMIAS
(hur.´mī.ahs)

(M) Several martyrs named HERMIAS are remembered by the Orthodox Church. St. HERMIAS, a soldier, suffered a martyr's death at Cappadocia in 170 A.D. The Orthodox Church commemorates the feasts of St. HERMIAS on November 4, May 31, and June 17.

HERMIONE
(hur.mī.ō.nē)

(F) This name from the Greek signifies "of the earth". Greek mythology gives us HERMOINE, the legendary daughter of Helen of Troy and Menelaus. In addition, HERMOINE is the daughter of the Apostle Philip. After the death of her father, HERMOINE traveled to Asia Minor in search of St. John the Evangelist. When she finally arrived in Ephesus, she found that St. John had died. Despite the fact, HERMOINE stayed and worked in the vineyard of Christ with Petronius, who was a fellow-worker of St. John. The Orthodox Church memorializes St. HERMOINE on September 4.

HESTER
(hes.turh)

(F) Variant forms of ESTHER. See ESTHER.

HESTHER
(hes.thuhr)

(F) Variant forms of ESTHER. See ESTHER.

HIERONYMUS
(hur.on.ē.muhs)

(M) The Greek equivalent of JEROME. See JEROME.

HILARA
(hil.ah.ra)

(F) Variant spelling of HILARIA. See HILARIA.

HILLAIRE
(hil.ār)

(F) Variant spelling of HILARIA. See HILARIA.

HILARIA
(hil.ar.ē.ah)

(F) Feminine form of HILARY. The Orthodox Church observes March 19, in memory of St. HILARIA.

HILARION
(hil.ar.ē.ohn)

(M) Variant spelling of HILARY. See HILARY.

HILARY
(hil.ah.rē)

(M/F) HILARY, in Greek means "cheerful; merry." In as much as, the name appears often on the Orthodox Church calendar, and the Church commemorates the memory of the martyrs named HILARY, the story of St. HILARY, the new martyr, is worthy of repeating. HILARY was under suspicion for stealing vast amounts of money in Constantinople. When he asked for assistance, the Turkish Sultan agreed to assist him, on the condition, that he would renounce his Christian faith and become a Moslem. HILARY agreed to this, but, soon after his conversion, he became repentant for his deed and took refuge at

Mt. Athos. His sincere repentance gave way to his sense of sin, and he returned to Constantinople, where he stood in the palace and confessed his faith in Jesus Christ. He was quickly beheaded on September 20, 1804.

HIRAM
(hī.́rahm)

(M) This name, HIRAM, is Hebrew from the Phoenician, which comes to us meaning "most noble," or "high born." The Old Testament tells of two men named HIRAM. In I Kings 5:1, HIRAM is a king of Tyre and a friend of David. Another HIRAM is a skilled worker, who supervised the decorating of the interior of Solomon's temple. (I Kings 7:13-45).

HOMER
(hō.́muhr)

(M) The meaning of this Greek name is "a pledge." The HOMER of ancient Greece is credited as being the author of **The Iliad** and **The Odyssey.**

HONOR, HONORA
(on.́uhr), (on.́or.ah)

(F) Variant forms of HONORIA. See HONORIA.

HONORIA
(on.or.́e.ah)

(F) "Honorable" is the Latin meaning of this name. Polytemi is the Greek equivalent.
A diminutive is Nora.

HOPE
(hōp)

(F) One of the three daughters of St. Sophia is named HOPE, (ELPIS) and the Orthodox Church remembers her, her mother, and sisters on September 17.

HOSEA
(hō.se.́ah)

(M) HOSEA is the prophet of the eighth century B.C. who authored the Old Testament book HOSEA. The Orthodox Church commemorates his memory on October 17.

HUMPHREY
(hum.́frē)

(M) Possible English equivalent of ONUPHRIUS. The Orthodox Church observes the memory of St. ONUPHRIUS on June 12.

HURAM
(hū.́rahm)

(M) Alternate form of HIRAM. See HIRAM.

HYACINTH
(hī.́ah.sinth)

(M/F) In Greek mythology, HYACINTH is the son of Anyclas, who was beloved by Apollo and Zepher. HYACINTH, who preferred Apollo, was killed by Zepher and HYACINTH'S blood became a flower. The petals are inscribed with "AI" which means "woe." (Virgil, **Eclogues** III, 106).

In addition, there is a Christian HYACINTH who was a teacher of Christian law. His memory is observed on June 3, in the Orthodox Church.

The name HYACINTH, originally, was a masculine name, however, it is rarely used as a masculine name and is used as a feminine name.

HYCINTH
(hī.sinth)

(M/F) Variant spelling of HYACINTH. See HYACINTH.

HYACINTHE
(hī.ah.sin.thē)

(M/F) Variant spelling of HYACINTH. See HYACINTH.

I

We go to gain a little patch of ground,
That hath in it no profit but the name.
Shakespeare, **HAMLET**

IAGO
(ē.a.gō)
(M) Welsh form for JAMES. See JAMES.

IAN, ION
(ē.'an), (ē.'ahn)
(M) The Scottish form of JOHN. See JOHN.

IANTHA
(ē.an.'thah)
(F) A "purple colored flower" is the meaning of IANTHA. IANTHA, according to OVID in **METAMORPHOSE**, is a Cretan maiden married to Iphis, who had been transformed from a girl to a young man so that they could marry.

IANTHE
(ē.an.'thā)
(F) A variant spelling of IANTHA. See IANTHA.

IANTHINA
(ē.an.thē.'nah)
(F) A variant spelling of IANTHA. See IANTHA.

ICARUS
(ik.'a.rus)
(M) In Greek mythology, ICARUS is the son of Daedalus. ICARUS did not heed his father's warning and flew too near the sun which melted the wax on his wings, and he fell to his death in the sea. The southeastern part of the Aegean Sea is named the Icarian Sea after ICARUS.

IDA
(ī.'dah)
(F) Mount IDA is very prominent in Greek mythology especially since there are two mountains which bear this name. The one in Crete, which is known now as "Psilorite", is connected with the most celebrated legends that are concerned with the infancy of Zeus. The other Mount Ida is in Asia Minor (Turkey) approximately thirty miles southeast of the plain of Troy. It was at this place that Ganymede was stolen, and where Paris served as judge in picking the "most fairest" goddess.

IDOLA
(ī.dol.'ah)
(F) "A lovely vision" is the Greek meaning of this name.

IGNACE, IGNATZ (ig.nãs), (ig.natz)	(M) Variant spellings of IGNATIUS. See IGNATIUS.
IGNACIA (ig.nã.se.ah)	(F) Feminine form of IGNATIUS. See IGNATIUS.
IGNATIA (ig.nã.shah)	(F) Variant forms of IGNACIA. See IGNATIUS.
IGNATZIA (ig.nat.zhah)	(F) Variant forms of IGNACIA. See IGNATIUS.
IGNATIUS (ig.nã.shuhs)	(M) The Latin translation is "fiery and ardent." The Orthodox Church commemorates the memory of several martyrs and saints named IGNATIUS, however, December 20, is reserved to honor the memory of IGNATIUS of Antioch. He is the Christian bishop and martyr known as "Theophorus."
ILKA (il.kah)	(F) Pet form from ILONKA. See ILONKA.
ILONKA, ILONA (i.lon.kah), (i.lo.nah)	(F) Hungarian form of HELEN. See HELEN.
IMMANUEL (e.man.u.ehl)	(M) A variant spelling of EMANUEL. See EMANUEL.
IMMANUELA (e.man.u.el.ah)	(F) A variant spelling of EMANUELA. See EMANUELA.
INEZ (i.nehz)	(F) This is the old Spanish and Portugese forms of AGNES. See AGNES.
IOAKIM (e.o.a.kem)	(M) The Russian form of JOACHIM. See JOACHIM.
IOCASTA (i.o.kas.tah)	(F) Variant spelling of JOCASTA. See JOCASTA.
IOLE (i.o.le)	(F) IOLE, of Greek mythology, is promised in marriage to Heracles by her father. When he reneged on his promise, Heracles merely picked her up and carried her away as his bride.
IONE (i.on)	(F) This Greek word means "purple jewel." The Orthodox Church observes August 22, in memory of St. IONE, martyr.
IPHAGENIA (if.a.je.ni.ah)	(F) "A beautiful sacrifice" is the translation of this name from Greek. In Greek mythology, IPHIGENIA is the daughter of Agamemnon and Clyteminestra. Her father offered her as a sacrifice for having offended Artemis, but, at the

last moment, Artemis snatched IPHEGENIA from the altar, and carried her to heaven.

Genia, Genie, and Igenea are diminutive forms.

IPHIGENIA
(if.uh.jē.nī.ah)

(F) Variant spelling of IPHIGENIA. See IPHIGENIA.

IPHIGENIAH
(if.a.jē.nī.a)

(F) Variant spelling of IPHIGENIA. See IPHIGENIA.

IRA
(ī.rah)

(M) IRA is Hebrew for "watchful."

IRENA
(e.rē.nah)

(F) A variant spelling of IRENE. See IRENE.

IRENE
(ī.rēen)

(F) The word IRENE, in Greek, means "peace." In ancient Greece, IRENE was worshipped as the goddess of peace, and because of its happy association, the name was adopted by Christians.

In the third century, when Diocletian ordered St. Sebastian to be shot to death with arrows for being a Christian, it was a pious woman named IRENE who tended his wounds after the archers failed in their attempt to execute him.

Another pious woman named IRENE, who gained sainthood and the title "Great among Martyrs," is remembered by the Orthodox Church on May 5. IRENE is the daughter of a governor and as a young girl she had a dream that she had been chosen to teach her people about Christ. In her mission to teach about Christ, she suffered many tortures, and was, finally, beheaded on May 5, 384 A.D.

Among the diminutive names are Renie, Rena, René, Rennie, Renny, and Nitsa.

IRINA
(e.rī.nah)

(F) The Russian form for IRENE. See IRENE.

IRIS
(ī.ruhs)

(F) In Greek mythology, IRIS is the goddess of the rainbow.

IRISA
(e.rē.sah)

(F) The Russian form for IRIS. See IRIS.

ISAAC
(ī.zak)

(M) In Hebrew, ISAAC means "laughter." ISAAC of the Old Testament is one of the patriarchal ancestors of the Hebrews and of Christ (Genesis 17:19; 18:12, 21:6). He is the son of Abraham and Sarah, and his memory is commemorated on the Sunday of Our Lord's Progenitors.

ISAAC, the Christian, suffered a martyr's death, and is memorialized on September 22, in the Orthodox Church.

ISABEL
(iz.'a.behl)

(F) Originally, the name ISABEL was derived from Babylonian and means "Oath to Baal." However, it became a Christian name when the Spanish used it for ELIZABETH. See ELIZABETH.

Belle and Bella are diminutive forms.

ISBEL
(īz.'behl)

(F) A variant spelling of ISABEL. See ISABEL.

ISADORA
(is.ah.dor.'ah)

(F) Feminine of ISADORE. The Orthodox Church commemorates the feasts of St. ISADORA on October 17, and May 1.

Diminutive forms include Dora, Dory, and Issy.

ISADORE
(iz.'a.dor)

(M) This Greek name can be interpreted in two ways. One meaning is "gift of Isis" and the other meaning is "equal gift." St. ISADORE, an officer in the army of Decius, was a Christian. When it was discovered that he was a Christian, he was ordered to deny Christ. He refused and was beheaded in 251 A.D. The Orthodox Church observes his feast day on May 14. There were other men named ISADORE, who achieved sainthood, and are remembered in the Orthodox Church on December 2, December 7, and February 4.

Dory, Issy, and Izzy are diminutive forms of the name.

ISAIAH
(ī.sā.'ah)

(M) The Hebrew translation is "salvation of the Lord." ISAIAH is a Hebrew prophet of the eighth century B.C., and is remembered by the Orthodox Church on the Sunday of Our Lord's Progenitors and on May 9.

ISIDORE
(is.'ah.dōr)

(M) A variant spelling of ISADORE. See ISADORE.

ISMAEL
(is.'mah.el)

(M) "God hears" is the Hebrew translation of this name. ISMAEL of the Old Testament is the son of Abraham and Hagar who is mistreated by Sarah. After the birth of Isaac, ISMAEL was driven from his home, and he took his mother Hagar to her native home of Egypt (Genesis 16;17).

A Christian ISMAEL gave his life for Christ, and the Orthodox Church observes June 17, in memory of St. Ismael, martyr.

ISMENE
(is'mēn)

(F) ISMENE is the loyal daughter of Oedipus and Jocasta and the sister of Antigone of Greek mythology.

IVAN
(ī'vuhn)

(M) The Russian form of JOHN. See JOHN.

J

JACENTA
(ja.sen.'tah)

(F) A variant spelling of JACINDA. See JACINDA.

JACINDA
(ja.sin.'dah)

(F) The interpretation of this Greek name is "beautiful, comely."

JACINTA
(ja.sin.'tah)

(F) Spanish form for HYACINTH. See HYACINTH.

JACOB
(ja.'kuhb)

(M) In Hebrew, the word means "to seize by the heel" or "to supplant." JACOB is the twin son of Isaac and Rebecca. The Orthodox Church memorializes JACOB on the Sunday of Our Lord's Progenitors.

A diminutive form of the name is Jake.

JACOBINA
(jak.ō.bin.'ah)

(F) Feminine form of JACOB. See JACOB.

JOCOVINA
(jō.kō.vē.'nah)

(F) Feminine form of JACOB. See JACOB.

JACQUELINE
(jak.'we.lin.)

(F) Feminine of French form for JACQUES. See JAMES.

JACQUES
(zhak)

(M) French form of JAMES. See JAMES.

JACQUETTA
(ja.kwē.'tah)

(F) A variant form of JACQUELINE. See JAMES

JAIME
(jā.'mē)

(M) Spanish form of JAMES. See JAMES.

JAMES
(jāmz)

(M) JAMES is a form of JACOB. In as much as, the Orthodox Church commemorates the memory of many saints named JAMES, there are three saints named JAMES who are of major impor-

86

tance. JAMES, the Apostle and brother of John the Theologian, is remembered on April 30; St. JAMES, the brother of the Lord and first Bishop, is commemorated on October 23, (this is the name-day of his Eminence Archbishop IAKOVOS); wherein JAMES, the Confessor, is honored on March 21.

There are numerous diminutives for JAMES, of which some are Jack, Jackie, Jimsey, Jamie, Jem, Jemmy, Jim, Jimmy and Jock.

JAN
(yan)

(M) The Dutch form of JOHN. See JOHN.

JANE
(jān)

(F) A feminine form of JOHN. See JOHN.

JANET
(ja.'nuht)

(F) A Scottish diminutive form of JANE from the French JEANETTE. See JOHN.

JANICE
(jan.'is)

(F) A form of JANE. See JOHN.

JANOS
(ya.'nōs)

(M) Hungarian form of JOHN. See JOHN.

JANTHINE
(jan.thīn)

(F) A variant form of IANTHE. See IANTHE.

JANUARIUS
(jan.'u.ar.ē.uhs)

(M) This name is derived from the name of the Roman god Janus, who was the god of beginnings, openings, entrances, doorways, and endings.

St. JANUARIUS, the martyr among priests, is remembered in the Orthodox Church on April 16.

JAOA
(zhōō.ouń)

(M) Portugese form of JOHN. See JOHN.

JAPHETH
(jā.'feth)

(M) In Hebrew, the word signifies "enlargement". JAPHETH is the eldest of Noah's three sons (Genesis 9:24; 10:21). The Orthodox Church commemorates his memory on the Sunday of Our Lord's Progenitors.

JARED
(jaŕ.id)

(M) The Hebrew word means "descent". JARED is the son of Maleleel and the father of Enoch, and the Orthodox Church observes his memory on the Sunday of Our Lord's Progenitors.

JASCHA
(ya.shah)

(M) The Russian diminutive form of JAMES. See JAMES.

JASMIN
(jas.'min)
JASMINE
(jas.'mīn)

(F) This Persian word means "fragrant flower." The Orthodox Church observes February 4, in memory of St. JASMINE the Righteous.

JASON
(jā.'sohn)

(M) The name JASON signifies "a healer" in Greek. In the mythology of the Greeks, JASON is the leader of the Argonants in quest of the Golden Fleece. The name JASON appears in Acts 17:5, and is written EASON. He is the Christian in Thessalonika and, perhaps, a relative of St. Paul, who shielded Paul from the rabble during Paul's first visit to Thessalonika (Acts 17:5-10). It seems that five years later, Jason was, also, with Paul at Corinth, (Romans 16:21). The Orthodox Church observes April 29 in his memory.

JASPER
(jas.'puhr)

(M) "Treasurer bringer" is the Persian meaning of this word, and truly, JASPER was a treasurer bringer for he is one of the Wise Men who went to Bethlehem to adore the Christ child.

The name evolved from Casper to Gasper to Jasper.

JAYNE
(jān)

(F) A variant spelling of JANE. See JOHN.

JEAN
(jēn)

(F) A diminutive from the French for JOANNA. See JOANNA.

JEANNE
(jēn)

French forms of JOANNA. See JOANNA.

JEANETTE
(jah.net)́

French forms of JOANNA. See JOANNA.

JEMIMA
(je.mī.'mah)

(F) In Hebrew, JEMIMA means "dove." JEMIMA is Job's daughter, the first of three born after his trials. (Job 42:14).

JEREMIAH,
JEREMIAS
(jer.'uh.mī.ah)
(jer.eh.mī.'ahs)

(M) "Exalted of the Lord" is the Hebrew translation. JEREMIAH is an Old Testament prophet of the sixth and seventh centuries B.C., and a book of the Old Testament bears his name. The Orthodox Church observes May 1, in his memory.

Jerry is a diminutive form of the name.

JEREMY
(jer.'uh.mē)

(M) A variant spelling of JEREMIAH. See JEREMIAH.

JEROME
(juh.rōm)́

(M) The name is derived from the Greek which means "the holy named." The name, in Greek, is

HIERONYMUS, which became JEROME in French. The Orthodox Church observes the memory of St. JEROME the Righteous on June 15.

Jerrie and Jerry are diminutive forms of JEROME.

JESAMINE
(jes:ah.min)

(F) Variant form of JASMINE. See JASMINE.

JESSAMY
(jes:ah.mē)

(F) Variant form of JASMINE. See JASMINE.

JESSE
(jes:ē)

(M) "Wealth" is the literal meaning of this Hebrew name. JESSE is the son of Obed, father of King David, and is referred to as "head of the house of David." He is memorialized in the Orthodox Church on the Sunday of Our Lord's Progenitors.

JESSICA
(jes:uh.ka)

(F) The name is from the Hebrew YISKAK which probably means "shut up" or "confined" (Genesis 11:29). The name appears as IESKA in Greek.

JOACHIM
(yō:a.khim) or
(yō.a:khim)

(M) "The Lord will judge" is the translation of this Hebrew word. JOACHIM is the name of the father of the Theotokos, and his memory is observed on September 9.

JOAN
(jōn)

(F) Another French feminine form of JOHN. See JOANNA.

JOANNA
(jō.an:ah)

(F) The feminine of JOHN. "Gracious gift of God" is the meaning of this Hebrew name. JOANNA is one of the ancestors of Jesus (Luke 3:27), and is memorialized on the Sunday of Our Lord's Progenitors.

Later in history, JOANNA is the name of one of the myrrh-bearing women, and her memory is solemnized on June 27, in the Orthodox Church.

JOAQUIN
(jā:kwin)

(M) Spanish form of JOACHIM. See JOACHIM.

JOB
(jōb)

(M) The JOB is from the Hebrew and means "one afflicted." JOB is the patriarch, who is noted for his integrity and piety. The Orthodox Church commemorates his memory on May 6.

JOCASTA
(jō.kas:tah)

(F) The Greek translation is "shining moon." JOCASTA is the Theban queen, of Greek legend, who unknowingly, married her son Oedipus.

JOEL
(jō.'uhl)

(M) This Biblical name implies "the Lord is God," and is the name of an Old Testament prophet. The Orthodox Church observes his memory on October 19.

JOHANAN
(jō.'an.ahn)

(F) A variant spelling of JOANNA. See JOANNA.

JOHANNES
(yō.'hanz)

(M) German form for JOHN. See JOHN.

JOHN
(jon)

(M) The English form of the Greek IOANES is from the Hebrew JOCHANAN meaning "God is gracious." The feminine form, JOANNA, is nearer to the original Hebrew word. The name JOHN is a very popular name, and there are more than fifty saints in the Orthodox Church who bear this name.

Among the saints with this name are:

St. JOHN the Evangelist, the "beloved disciple," who took the Theotokos to Ephesus after the Crucifixion. At Ephesus he was persecuted, so he went to the isle of Patmos where he wrote the Book of Revelations. He died at Ephesus at a very advanced age. The Orthodox Church memorializes him on May 8.

St. JOHN the Baptist who was sent "to prepare the way of the Lord" is memorialized several times. One of the days reserved for his memory is January 7.

St. JOHN CHRYSOSTOM "The golden mouthed" is one of the four Doctors of the Church. As a priest and Patriarch of Constantinople, he did much to purify the Church, but his enemies had him exiled. For his holiness, his eloquent sermons, and his liturgical reforms, he is remembered, and the Orthodox Church memorializes him on November 13, and January 30.

Diminutives of the name are Jack, Johnny, Jonny, and Zane.

JONAS
(jō.'nahs)

(M) The Hebrew word for "dove" is JONA or JONAH, but in Matthew 12:39-41, the name JONAH took the Greek form JONAS. JONAS is a prophet in the Old Testament, and in the New Testament, JONAS is the father of Peter and Andrew (John 21:15-17). The Orthodox Church observes September 21, in memory of both

JONAS the prophet and St. JONAS the Righteous.

JONATHAN
(joń.uh.thahn)

(M) This Biblical name from the Hebrew is translated as "gift of Jehovah." JONATHAN is the eldest son of Saul and the loyal friend of David (I Samuel 21:7). His friendship for David is one of the most beautiful friendships in the Old Testament. The Orthodox Church remembers JONATHAN on the Sunday of Our Lord's Progenitors.

A diminutive form is Jon.

JORDAN
(jordń)

(M) JORDAN is the name of the river in Palestine where St. John the Forerunner baptized Jesus. The word is from the Hebrew "flowing down". The Orthodox Church commemorates the memory of St. JORDAN, the miracle worker, on May 2.

JORGE
(jorgí)

(M) Spanish form for GEORGE. See GEORGE.

JOSEPH
(jō.zef)

(M) "He shall add" is the Hebrew meaning of JOSEPH. There are many pious men named JOSEPH who are memorialized in the Orthodox Church, but there are three who are notable. JOSEPH of the Old Testament, who had a coat of many colors, (Genesis 37:3) is remembered on October 30. St. JOSEPH, the husband of the Theotokos, who is a descendent of the House of David, is commemorated on the Sunday after Christmas. The Orthodox Church memorializes St. JOSEPH of Arimathea on July 31. St. JOSEPH is remembered for giving Christ the proper burial.

Diminutive forms are Joe and Joey.

JOSEPHA
(jō.sef.ah)

(F) Feminine forms of JOSEPH. See JOSEPH. Josie and Jo are diminutive forms.

JOSEPHINE
(jō.se.fēn)

(F) Feminine forms of JOSEPH. See JOSEPH. Josie and Jo are diminutive forms.

JOSHUA
(josh.ōō.ah)

(M) The name JOSHUA is from the Hebrew and is translated as "the Lord is salvation." JOSHUA, of the Old Testament, is a leader of the Israelites after the death of Moses.

JOSIAS
(jō.sī.uhs)

(M) "Jehovah saves" is the meaning in Hebrew. JOSIAS is an ancestor of Our Lord (Luke 3:31.)

JOSIP (zhṓ.suhp)	(M) The Serbian form of JOSEPH. See JOSEPH.
JOVAN (zhṓ.van)	(M) The Serbian form of JOHN. See JOHN.
JOY (joi)	(F) The English equivalent of CHARA. See CHARA.
JUAN (whan)	(M) The Spanish form for John. See JOHN.
JUDE (jōōd)	(M) This is the English form of Judas. See THADDEUS.
JUDITH (joo.́dith)	(F) This name has two possible meanings. From the Hebrew, it means "admired; praised," and from the Greek, it is the feminine of "a Jew." The name JUDITH first appears in Genesis 26:34, as the wife of Esau, and she is remembered in the Orthodox Church on the Sunday of Our Lord's Progenitors. The name also appears in the Apocrypha as the Book of Judith. Diminutives are Jody and Judy.
JULES, JULIEN (joolz), (jool.́yehn)	(M) Variant forms of JULIUS. See JULIUS.
JULIA (jōōl.́yah)	(F) The feminine form of JULIUS. JULIA is the Christian woman at Rome to whom St. Paul sent greetings (Romans 16:15). The Orthodox Church observes the memory of St. JULIA, the martyr, on May 18. Jill is a diminative form.
JULIAN (jōōl.́yahn)	(M) The name JULIAN is from the Latin and means "sprung from or belonging to JULIUS." The Orthodox Church celebrates the memory of St. JULIAN, the Egyptian, on June 21. Other men named JULIAN also gave their lives for Christ and the Orthodox Church honors them on October 7, September 2, 4, 12, January 8, February 5, and March 6 and 16.
JULIANA, (jōō.lē.an.́ah), JULIANE (jōō.lē.an)́	(F) Variant forms of JULIA. The Orthodox Church remembers St. JULIANE of Nikomedia on December 21.
JULIETTA (jōōl.́et.ah)	(F) Variant form of JULIA. The martyr St. JULIETTA is remembered by the Orthodox Chruch on July 15.

JULIUS
(jōōl.yuhs)

(M) The name JULIUS is the name of a Roman gens. The centurian JULIUS had great respect for St. Paul (Acts 27). See JULIAN.

JUNE
(jōōn)

(F) This name is from JUNO the Roman goddess. JUNIA is one of Paul's kinsmen in Rome (Romans 9:3), who received title "apostle" by the Church. Her memory is solemnized in the Orthodox Church on May 17.

JUSTA
(jus.tah)

(F) This is Latin for "just". The Orthodox Church remembers St. JUSTA the Righteous on April 26.

JUSTIN
(jus.tin)

(M) The Latin translation of JUSTIN is "just." The Orthodox Church commemorates the memory of St. JUSTIN, the philosopher, on June 1. JUSTIN is the Palestinian Greek philosopher who was deeply imbeded with Stoic and Platonic ideas. When he discovered Christianity, he spent the remainder of his life traveling and teaching about Christ and Christianity. JUSTIN established a school in Rome, but was executed under Marcus Aurelius in 155 A.D.

JUSTINA
(jus.te.nah)

(F) The feminine form of JUSTIN. St JUSTINA, the martyr, is remembered on October 2, in the Orthodox Church.

JUSTINIAN
(jus.tin.e.ahn)

(M) A form of JUSTIN. Emperor JUSTINIAN the Great's greatest accomplishments was his Code of Civil Law, which was the only legislative code until that time. He also was the Emperor who commissioned the building of the Great Church of St. Sophia (Holy Wisdom) in Constantinople.

The Orthodox Church celebrates his memory on November 15, and August 2.

JUSTUS
(jus.tuhs)

(M) Masculine form of JUSTA. The name JUSTUS appears three times in the New Testament. It is the name of Joseph, surnamed Barnabas (Acts 1:23); JUSTUS is the Corinthian convert, in whose house Paul preached (Acts 18:7); and finally, JUSTUS is the Jewish convert who was a fellow-laborer with Paul and Mark at Rome. (Colossians 4:11). The Orthodox Church remembers JUSTUS, the apostle, on October 30.

K

Their bodies are buried in peace; but their name liveth for evermore.
Ecclesiasticus 44:14

KALIMACHOS
(ka.lim.'ah.kohs)

(M) "Good battle" is the Greek meaning of this name. St. KALIMACHOS is remembered on November 7, in the Orthodox Church.

KANELLA
(ka.nel.'lah)

(F) The Greek meaning of this name is "cinnamon." The diminutive Ella may be used for this name.

KAREN
(kar.'ehn)

(F) The Scandinavian form of KATHERINE. See KATHERINE.

KARSTEN
(kar.'stuhn)

(M) This masculine name is derived from the Greek, which means "the Christian; the blessed one." see CHRISTIAN.

A diminutive form is Kirt.

KATHERINE
KATHERINE
(kath.'ah.rin),
(kath.'eh.rin)

(F) The name KATHERINE has its roots in the Greek word "Katheros" which means "pure". The name goes back to the Greek form AIKATERINE.

St. KATHERINE of Alexandria was a member of a noble or royal family of Alexandria, Egypt or perhaps, of Cyprus. KATHERINE was in her teens when she accepted Christ and was baptized. Shortly after her baptism, she had a vision of her mystical espousal with Christ. During a persecution, she was seized in Alexandria. At her trial, she converted fifty philosophers, the empress, and 200 members of the guard. She was convicted, tortured on a spiked wheel, and finally, beheaded on November 24 or 25, 305 A.D. The Orthodox Church solemnizes the feast of St. KATHERINE on November 25.

Some of the diminutive forms of the name include Cassie, Cathy, Kate, Kit, Kitty, Ina, Kara, Kathie, Katie, Trina, Kay, Kathe, and Kathy.

KATHLEEN (kath.'lēn)	(F) The Irish form of KATHERINE. See KATHERINE.
KATHLENE (kath.'lēn)	(F) The Irish form of KATHERINE. See KATHERINE.
KATHYRNE (kath.'ern)	(F) Variant spelling of KATHERINE. See KATHERINE.
KATINA (ka.tē.'nah)	(F) Diminutive form of KATHERINE. See KATHERINE.
KATINKA (ka.tin.'kah)	(F) Diminutive form of KATHERINE. See KATHERINE.
KATRINA (ka.trē.'nah)	(F) Diminutive form of KATHERINE. See KATHERINE.
KERIAKE (ker.'ē.a.kē)	(F) This name is from the Greek, "The Lord's Day." It was the custom of the Greeks to bestow the name KERIAKE on a girl if she was born on "the Lord's Day" or rather, Sunday. Boys born on Sunday were named KERIAKOS. The Latin names DOMINICA and DOMINIC can be used for the English equivalent of the names KERIAKE and KERIAKOS. There are saints named KERIAKE, and the Orthodox Chruch observes July 7, for the St. KERIAKE who professed her faith to God rather than to the pagan gods, and she gave her life for Christ. Kerry is a diminutive of the name.
KERIAKOS (ker.ē.a.'kuhs)	(M) Masculine form of KERIAKE. See K E R I A K E .
KESTER (kes.'tehr)	(M) Diminutive form of CHRISTOPHER. See CHRISTOPHER.
KHRISTOS (kris.'tohs)	(M) Variant Spelling of CHRISTOS. See CHRISTOS.
KIKI (kē.'kē)	(F) Greek feminine diminutive of names such as Angeliki, Basikiki.
KIMON (kimóhn)	(M) A distinguished general and statesman of ancient Greece.
KIRSTEN (kir.'stuhn)	(M) A variant spelling KARSTEN. See CHRISTIAN.
KORA (kor.'ah)	(F) Variant spelling of CORA. See CORA.

KOSTAS
(kos.tahs)

(M) The Greek diminutive for CONSTANTINE.

KRISTEN
(kris.tehn)
KRISTIN
(kris.tihn)

(F) Early Greeks bestowed this name on their new-born daughters to honor Christ Our Lord. The name has its roots in CHRISTINA "follower of Christ".

KRISTIAN
(kris.chahn)

(M) A variant spelling of CHRISTIAN. See CHRISTIAN.

L

LACHESIS
(lak.'e.sihs)

(F) LACHESIS is one of the three Fates in Greek mythology who was the Disposer of Lots. It was she who assigned to each his/her destiny.

LAKIS
(la.'kēs)

(M) Greek diminutive form for masculine names such as BASIL - BASILAKIS. See AKIS.

LAMBRENE
(lam.'brēn)

(F) Feminine of LAMBROS. The Latin names CLARA or CLARICE can be used for a more correct translation of the name LAMBRENE, since CLARA means "bright" in Latin.

LAMBROS
(lam.'brōs)

(M) "Splendid, brilliant" is the meaning of this name in Greek. Easter is referred to as LAMBRE and those named LAMBROS, most generally, celebrate their feast day on Easter Sunday. In addition to this feast day, the feast of St. LAMBROS, the neo-martyr, is observed on July 2.

PASCAL is the English equivalent of LAMBROS.

LARISIA
(la.ris.'i.ah)

(F) The Greek translation is "cheerful maiden."

LARISSA
(la.ris.'ah)

(F) Variant form of LARISIA. See LARISIA.

LAURA
(lor.'ah)

(F) In as much as, the word LAURA, from the Latin, may mean "the laurel" or it might be from "l'aura - the air," the word appears in the Ionic dialect of ancient Greek and is translated as "an alley, a lane, or a narrow passage between houses." In this context then, some early monasteries consisted of separate cells under a superior, and the occupants of these cells met only for chapel services and for a common meal in the dining hall. This type of monastery was called a "LAURA". The modern Greek meaning of LAURA is "burning, heat, ardor."

A St. LAURA is remembered by the Orthodox Church on August 18.

A few diminutives derived from this name are Lora, Lori, Lorie, and Lorrie.

LAURALIE
(lor.'a.lĭ)

(F) Variant of LAURA. See LAURA.

LAUREEN
(lor.ēn)́

(F) Variant of LAURA. See LAURA.

LAUREN
(lor.'ehn)

(F) Variant of LAURA. See LAURA.

LAURENCE
LAWRENCE
(lor.'ens), (lar.'ens)

(M) This name is from the Latin and signifies "of or belonging to Lawrentum, a town in Litium."

St. LAWRENCE, who was persecuted by being roasted alive by Valerian, refused to turn over the Church's treasury when the governor demanded it. Instead, St. LAWRENCE pointed to the widows and orphans and said, "Behold! the treasure of the Church". The Orthodox Church remembers St. LAWRENCE The Righteous on May 10.

Lanny, Larry, Laro, and Lorry comprise some of the diminutive forms.

LAURENT
(lor.'ehnt)

(M) Variant form of LAWRENCE. See LAWRENCE.

LAWRENCIA
(la.ren.'shē.ah)

(F) Feminine of LAWRENCE. See LAWRENCE.

LAZARUS
(la.'za.ruhs)

(M) The Hebrew name implies "help of God." The Graeco-Latin form of this Hebrew name is ELEAZAR.

The name LAZARUS appears in the New Testament as the brother of Mary and Martha of Bithany whom Christ restored to life (John 11:4). The Orthodox Church commemorates this event on the Saturday of Lazarus--the Saturday prior to Palm Sunday. The names LAZARUS appears again, in the New Testament, as the beggar who laid at the rich man's gate. (Luke 16:20).

LEAH
(lē.'a)

(F) This word, which is probably Hebrew, signifies "weary." LEAH is the first wife of JACOB. (Genesis 29:16-23). The Orthodox Church remembers LEAH on the Sunday of Our Lord's Progenitors.

LEANDER

(M) "Lion man" is the definition of this Greek

| (lē.an.'dehr) | word. LEANDER, in mythology, is the youth who loved Hero, and swam the Hellespont (modern day Dardenelles) each night to be with her. |

Diminutives are Lee and Andy.

LEDA
(lē.'dah)

(F) The meaning of this word in Greek is "woman." LEDA, of Greek mythology, is the queen of Sparta and mother of Castor and Clytemnestra.

LENA
(lē.'nah)

(F) A diminutive form of HELENA. See HELENA.

LEO
(lē.'ō)

(M) Variant of the name LEON. See LEON.

LEON
(le.'on)

(M) This name means "lion." Several men named LEON are remembered by the Orthodox Church for their work in the vineyard of Christ. The feasts of St. LEON Patriarch is solemnized on November 12; St. LEON, the bishop, is kept on February 20; St. LEON, martyr, is observed on January 22, February 18, and August 18; and St. LEON, neomartyr, is kept on July 1.

LEONARD
(len.'ahrd)

(M) The German form of LEONIDAS. See LEONIDAS.

LEONIDAS
(lē.ō.nī.'duhs)

(M) "Lion-like" is the meaning of this Greek word, LEONIDAS is the king of Sparta, who defended the pass at Thermopylae against the Persians in 480 B.C.

A Christian man named LEONIDAS gave his life for Christ, and the Orthodox Church observes the feast of St. LEONIDAS ON June 5.

LEONTIS
(lē.on.'tuhs)

(M) "Lion" is the definition of this Greek word. St. LEONTIS, bishop of Caesarea, was one of the fathers at the Council of Nicaea 325 A.D. The Orthodox Church observes his memory on May 14.

LEUCOTHE,
LEUCOTHEA
(lu.koth.'ē)
(lu.koth.'ē.ah)

(F) The definition of LEUCOTHEA is "white goddess." In Greek mythology, Cadmus and Athamas had a daughter, Ino, who became a sea goddess and was called LEUCOTHEA.

LEVI
(lē.'vī)

(M) LEVI means "joining" in Hebrew.

A LEVI is an ancestor of Jesus (Luke 3:24), and the Orthodox Church remembers him on the Sunday of Our Lord's Progenitors. Another LEVI is the third son of Jacob, and founder of a tribe

(Hebrew 7:5,9). In addition, there is another LEVI, son of Alphaeus, who is also called Matthew, the disciple of Our Lord. (see Matthew).

LILIKA
(lē.lē.́kah)

(F) This name is from the Latin "liluim-lily flower."

LILLIAN
(lil.́i.uhn)

(F) Diminutive of ELIZABETH. See ELIZABETH.

LIONEL
(lī.́uh.nuhl)

(M) A variant of LEON. See LEON.

LINIS, LINUS
(lī.́nuhs), (lī.́nuhs)

(M) "Flaxen-haired" is the Greek meaning of LINUS. Although LINUS appears in mythology as the minstrel son of Apollo and Urania, there is, also, a Christian LINUS. He is the Christian, in Rome, whose greetings Paul sent to Timothy (II Timothy 4:21). The Orthodox Church commemorates his memory on November 5.

LOIS
(lō.́ihs)

(F) The exact meaning of this word is not known, but it is probable that it may be interpreted as "battle maiden."

LOIS, Timothy's grandmother, is mentioned only once in the Bible in II Timothy 1:5.

LOLLIA
(lō.́lyah)

(F) The Orthodox Church observes the memory of St. LOLLIA martyr on June 23.

LONGINUS
(lon.́jin.uhs)

(M) LONGINUS is the name traditionally given to the centurion who pierced the side of the crucified Christ with a lance. The name is derived from the Greek word "longche" which means "lance." After Christ's crucifixion, LONGINUS became an apostle of Our Lord, and suffered a martyr's death. The Orthodox Church commemorates his day on October 16.

LORALIE
(lor.́a.lī)

(F) Variant form of LAURA. See LAURA.

LORELIE
(loráh.lē)

(F) Variant form of LAURA. See LAURA.

LOREN
(lor.́uhn)

(F) Variant form of LAURA. See LAURA.

LORENZ
(lor.́enz)

(M) Variant form of LAWRENCE. See LAWRENCE.

LORENZO
(lor.́en.zō)

(M) Variant form of LAWRENCE. See LAWRENCE.

LORETTE, LORIN (F) Variant forms of LAURA.
(lor.et), (lor.uhn)

LORINDA (F) Variant form of LAURA.
(lor.in.dah)

LORINE, LORNA (F) Variant forms of LAURA.
(lor.ēn), (lor.nah)

LORNE (F) Variant form of LAURA.
(lorn)

LUCAS, LUKE (M) In Greek, LUKE means "wolf." The name
(lōō.kahs), (lōōk) Lukas may be the abbreviated pet form of either Lukanos or Lukios.

LUKE is the name of the third Evangelist, a Greek of Antioch, who was a physician by profession. He became a fellow worker of St. Paul, and stayed with him until Paul's martyrdom. In Colossians 4:14, Paul refers to Luke as "the glorious physician." There is no evidence that he died a martyr's death. The Orthodox Church commemorates his memory on October 18.

LUCIA, LUCINA (F) Feminine of LUCIAN. This name is from the
(lōō.shah), Latin "lux" which means "light". An archaic
(lōō.sī.nah) meaning of LUCINA is "a midwife." LUCINA is the Roman goddess of childbirth, and the word has its roots in the Latin word "licinus," which means "to bring to light."

St. LUCIA is the virgin martyr whose memory is observed on December 13, in the Orthodox Church.

Lu, Luce, Lucie, and Lucy are diminutives.

LUCIAN (M) "Belonging to or sprung from Lucius" is the
(lōō.shahn) Latin translation of this name.

LUCIAN is the name of a Cyrene, an early Christian in the Church of Antioch (Acts 13:1). Also, in the third century, a man LUCIAN was martyred during the reign of the Roman Emperor Maximian. The Orthodox Church honors St. LUCIAN on October 15.

LUCILE (F) Variant form of LUCIA. See LUCIA.
(lōō.sēl)

LUCILLA (F) Variant form of LUCIA. See LUCIA.
(lōō.sil.ah)

LUCILLE (F) Variant form of LUCIA. See LUCIA.
(lōō.sēl)

LUCINDA (loo.sin.dah)	(F) Variant form of LUCIA. See LUCIA.
LUCY (loo.se)	(F) Variant form of LUCIA. See LUCIA.
LYCIA (lish.e.ah)	(F) Variant spelling of LUCY. See LUCY.
LYDIA (lid.e.ah)	(F) The name LYDIA has two meanings in Greek. It may indicate "a native of Lydia, in Asia Minor," or it may mean "cultured." LYDIA is mentioned in the Bible in Acts 16:14. She is the woman of Thyatira, who resided at Philippi, and dealt with purple cloth. Although she was not Jewish by birth, she became a convert to Judaism, and was led, by the grace of God, to be Paul's first European convert. Her memory is commemorated on March 27, in the Orthodox Church.
LYKERIA (li.ker.e.ah)	(F) Feminine of LYCURGUS. The Orthodox Church observes the martyrdom of St. LYKERIA on July 7. A diminutive form is Kerry.
LYCURGUS (li.kur.guhs)	(M) The translation of this name from Greek is "killer of wolves." The name appears at two different times in the ancient history of Greece. LYCURGUS, of the ninth century B.C., is the Spartan lawgiver, and the LYCURGUS, of the fourth century B.C., is one of the Ten Attic orators who was a pupil of Plato and Isocrates.

M

We toil for fame,
We live on crusts,
We make a name,
Then we are busts,
  L. H. Robbins

MACARIUS
(mak.́ah.rē.uhs)

(M) The name MACARIUS means "blissful" in Greek. The Orthodox Church observes the memory of St. MACARIUS the Egyptian on January 19.

MACRINA
(mak.rē.́nah)

(F) "Distant; far" is the translation of this name from Greek. St. MACRINA is the paternal grandmother of S. S. Basil and Gregory of Nyssa. St. MACRINA's granddaughter, also named MACRINA, helped her parents in training her ten younger brothers and sisters. When they were grown, MACRINA, then, became a nun. The feast of St. MACRINE is memorialized on July 19, in the Orthodox Church.

Rina is a diminutive form.

MADALEIN
(mad.́ah.lin)

(F) Variant of the French form for MAGDALEN. See MAGDALEN.

MADELENE
(mad.́ah.lēn)

(F) Variant of the French form for MAGDALEN. See MAGDALEN.

MADELINE
(mad.́ah.lı̄n)

(F) Variant of the French form for MAGDALEN. See MAGDALEN.

MADELON
(mad.́ah.lon)

(F) Variant of the French form for MAGDALEN. See MAGDALEN.

MADONNA
(ma.don.́ah)

(F) The English equivalent of PANAGIOTA. This is Italian for "my lady" and is a title especially applied to the Theotokos-the Virgin Mary.

Donna is a diminutive form.

MAGDALA,
MAGDALEN

(F) MAGDALEN is derived from the Hebrew, which means "belonging to Magdala" or "a

(mag.́da.lah) (mag.́da.len)	tower of strength." See MARY MAGDELINE. Diminutives includes Mada, Magda, Maud, Maudlin, and Lena.
MAISIE (mā.́zē)	(F) Scottish variant of MARGARET. See MARGARET.
MALACHAI (mal.́ah.kī)	(M) In Hebrew, MALACHAI means "messenger of Jehovah." He is one of the Minor Prophets of the Old Testament, and he foretold of the coming of John the Baptist and of the coming of Christ. (Malachai 3:1; 4:5-6). The Orthodox Church commemorates the memory of MALACHAI on January 3.
MALAN (Mā.́lahn)	(F) Variant of MELANIE. See MELANIE.
MANUEL (man.́ū.el)	(M) Diminutive of EMMANUEL. See EMMANUEL. Several men named MANUEL gave their lives for Christ, and the Orthodox Church observes their memory on January 22, March 26, and June 17.
MANUELA (man.́ū.el.ah)	(F) Feminine form of MANUEL. See EMMANUEL.
MARA (mar.́ah)	(F) Diminutive of DAMARA. See DAMARA.
MARC, MARK (mark), (mark)	(M) "Belonging to Mars;" "a warrior," is the Latin derivation of this name. St. Mark, the writer of one of the four Gospels, died in prison c. 68 A.D. The Orthodox Church observes his memory on April 25.
MARCEL (mar.sel)́	(M) Variant spelling of MARCELLUS. See MARCELLULS.
MARCELA (mar.sel.́ah)	(F) Feminine of MARCELLUS. The feast of St. MARCELLA is observed on July 22. Marcy, Marcie, and Marsha comprise the diminutives.
MARCELLA (mar.sel.́ah)	(F) Feminine of MARCELLUS. The feast of St. MARCELLA is observed on July 22. Marcy, Marcie, and Marsha comprise the diminutives.
MARCELLUS (mar.sel.́uhs)	(M) The name MARCELLUS is Latin and means "of Mars". Several men named MARCELLUS died a martyr's death for Christ, and are

remembered in the Orthodox Church on November 15, December 29, February 9, and March 1.

MARCIA
(mar.shah)

(F) Feminine form of MARK. The Orthodox Church observes June 9, 27, in memory of St. MARCIA, the martyr.

MARCIAN
(mar.shuhn)

(M) Variant form of MARK. MARCIAN, a native of Constantinople, was ordained a priest, and appointed treasurer of the church of St. Sophia. In this capacity, he supervised the building of several churches, notably the church of St. Anastasis in Constantinople.

The Orthodox Church observes his memory on January 10.

MARGARET
(marg.ah.ret)

(F) "Pearl" is the translation of this name from the Greek. In the 3rd century, St. MARGARET, who along with Sts. Barbara, Agnes, and Katherine, became one of the four virgin martyrs. St. MARGARET is known as St. MARINA in the Orthodox Church, and her feast is celebrated on July 17.

There are many variant spellings which have generated numerous diminutives, of which some are Greta, Meg, Madge, Maggie, Margie, Marjory, Meta, Peg, Peggy, and Rita.

MARGARETE
(mar.gah.ret)

(F) Variant form of MARGARET. See MARGARET.

MARGARITA
(mar.gah.re.tah)

(F) Variant form of MARGARET. See MARGARET.

MARGUERITA
(mar.ger.e.tah)

(F) Variant form of MARGARET. See MARGARET.

MARGO, MARGOT
(mar.go), (mar.go)

(F) Variant forms of MARGARET. See MARGARET.

MARIA
(ma.re.ah)

(F) The name MARIA is of doubtful origin and meaning. Some authorities suggest that the name is from the Hebrew and means "sorrowful; bitter," while others indicate it means "wished-for-child" or "rebellion." However, it is one of the oldest and most significant names in the Christian Church. The name of the Theotokos is MARIA, and the Orthodox Church honors her on September 8-the birth of the Theotokos; November 21-Presentation to the Temple; March

25-The Annunciation; and August 15-The Repose of the Theotokos.

Other saints who bear the name MARIA are also honored in the Orthodox Church, such as MARIA, sister of Lazarus, is remembered on June 16, and MARIA of Egypt on April 1.

MARIAN, MARIE (mar.ē.ahń), (mar.ē) (F) French forms of MARIA. See MARIA.

MARIANNE (mar.ē.an) (F) The name MARIANNE is a compound of MARY and ANNE.

MARIKA (ma.rē.kah) (F) A diminutive form of MARY. See MARIA.

MARILYN (mar.ah.lin) (F) This name is probably a diminutive form of MARY. See MARIA.

MARINA (ma.rē.nah) (F) From the Latin, this name signifies "sea maiden." The Orthodox Church observes July 17, the feast day of St. MARINA the Great Martyr. See MARGARET.

A diminutive form is Rina.

MARIO (mar.ē.ō) (M) Italian masculine form of MARY. MARIO is a closer equivalent of the Greek name Panagiotes than any of the other names that are currently used in the mistranslation of the name.

MARION (mar.ē.uhn) (M) The masculine form of MARY. The Orthodox Church remembers St. MARION, the deacon, on March 19.

MARIS, MARRAS (mar.uhs), (mar.as) (M) This name, from the Latin, is translated as "sea star." The Orthodox Church observes January 25, in memory of St. MARIS the Righteous.

MARISSA (ma.ris.ah) (F) The feminine form of MARIS. See MARIS.

MARLA (mar.lah) (F) This is a derivition of the name MARY. See MARIA.

MARLEEN (mar.lēn) (F) Variant spellings of MADELINE. See MADELINE.

MARLENE (mar.lēn) (F) Variant spellings of MADELINE. See MADELINE.

MARLINE (mar.lin) (F) Variant spellings of MADELINE. See MADELINE.

MARON (ma.rohn)	(M) In Greek history, MARON is the Spartan who distinguished himself at Thermopylae. The memory of the Christian MARON, St. MARON the Righteous, is observed on February 14, in the Orthodox Church.
MARSHA (mar.'shah)	(F) Variant of MARCIA.
MARTA (mar.'ta)	(F) This is the form of MARTHA which is used in Italy and Spain. See MARTHA.
MARTELLA (mar.tel.'ah)	(F) A variant form of MARTHA see MARTHA.
MARTHA (mar.'thah)	(F) The ancient Aramaic language provided this name, which means "the lady; mistress." MARTHA is the sister of St. Lazarus and St. Mary Magdalene (Luke 10:38; John 11:5). The Orthodox Church observes her memory on June. 4. Martie, Matti, and Mattie are among the diminutives.
MARTIN (mar.'tehn)	(M) MARTIN is a form of the name MARK. Several saints, who are named MARTIN, are honored in the Orthodox Church. St. MARTIN the Righteous is commemorated on April 13. St. MARTIN, the bishop, on November 12, and St. MARTIN, the martyr, on September 22.
MARTINA (mar.te.'nah)	(F) Feminine form of MARTIN. See MARTIN.
MARTYN (mar.'tin)	(M) A variant spelling of MARTIN. See MARTIN.
MARY (mar.'ĩ)	(F) This is a form of MARIA. See MARIA.
MARY MAGDALENE (mar.'ē mag.dah.lēn)	(F) See MARIA and MAGDALENE. MARY MAGADLENE is one of the myrrh-bearing women, and the Orthodox Church commemorates her memory on the second Sunday after Easter, and again on July 22.
MATHIAS, MATTHAIS (ma.thī.'uhs) (ma.thā.'uhs)	(F) MATHIAS is the Apostle, chosen by lot, to take the place left by the traitor, Judas Iscariot (Acts 1:26). The name is the shortened form of MATTATHIAS. His memory is observed on August 9, in the Orthodox Church.
MATRONA (ma.trō.'nah)	(F) The Latin translation indicates the meaning "of the mother; motherly." MATRONA, a ser-

vant of a rich Jewess of Thessalonika, was martyred at the instigation of her mistress. March 27, is observed as the feast of St. MATRONA the Righteous, in the Orthodox Church.

Ronna and Tronna are the diminutive forms.

MATTHEW
(math.yōō)

(M) From the Hebrew, this name expresses "gift of Jehovah." MATTHEW is the revenue officer who, then, became one of the Twelve Disciples of Christ. He is credited with writing the first book of the New Testament. The Orthodox Church commemorates the feast of St. Matthew the Evangelist on November 16.

Diminutives of this name are Maddie, Mat, Matt, and Matty.

MAURA
(ma.rah)

(F) Feminine form of MAURICE. St. MAURA, a maiden, was martyred at Constantinople, and one of the Ionian islands is named for her. The Orthodox Church commemorates her memory on May 3.

MAUREEN
(mau.rēn)

(F) The Irish form of MARY is "Mairin," and this is a diminutive form of the Irish name. See MARIA.

MAURICE
(mau.ris)

(M) This name is from the Latin meaning "Moorish; dark colored." The martyr, St. MAURICE, is remembered on December 27, in the Orthodox Church.

Diminutives include Maurey, Maury and Morrey.

MAUROS
(mau.rohs)

(M) A variant spelling of MAURICE. See MAURICE.

MAXIMILIAN,
MAXIMILLIAN
(maks.uh.mil.yahn)
(maks.uh.mil.yahn)

(M) The name is from the Latin, and is a combination of "maximus" and "aemilianus" which is understood to mean "the greatest Aemilianus." Several named MAXIMILIAN achieved sainthood, and are remembered in the Orthodox Church on October 22, and August 4.

Max is the diminutive form.

MAXINE
(maks.ēn)

(F) Feminine of MAXIMILIAN. See MAXIMILIAN.

MELAN
(mē.ahn)
MELANA
(me.lan.ah)

(F) Variant form of MELANIE. See MELANIE.

(F) Variant form of MELANIE. See MELANIE.

MELANIA,
MELANIE
(me.lan.'ah),
(me.lan.'e.ah)

(F) The translation, from the Greek, is "darkness; clad in black." The Orthodox Church commemorates the memory of St. MELANIE the Righteous on December 31.

Mel, Mellie, and Melly are the diminutive forms.

MELANTHE
(mel.an.'the)

(F) "Dark flower" is the meaning of this Greek name. This, probably, refers to a deep purple lily that once grew on the Mediterranean shores.

MELETIUS
(me.let.'e.uhs)

(M) St. MELETIUS is honored in the Orthodox Church on February 12. He was ordained a deacon by St. John Chrysostom and served as his deacon. MELETIUS became Archbishop of Antioch c. 360 during the Arian controversy. In a short while, he was exiled by the Arian emperor, recalled, and banished again. In 381, MELETIUS presided over the Second Council of Constantinople, and died on February 12, 382 A.D., while the Council was in session. The Orthodox Church commemorates his memory on Feburary 12.

MELINA
(mel.in.'ah)

(F) "Gentle" is the translation of this Greek word.

MELISSA
(mel.is.'ah)

(F) The Greek word for "honey bee" is MELISSA. MELISSA, the daughter of King Melissus of Crete, gathered goat's milk for the infant Zeus. She learned to gather honey from the bees, and was turned into a honey bee.

The diminutives for this name are Mel, Lisa, Lissa, and Missy.

MELITA
(me.le.'tah)

(F) "Little honey flower" is the Greek meaning of this name.

MELITINA
MELITINE
(mel.uh.te.'nah),
(mel.uh.tin)

(F) St. Melitina is the maiden who was martyred at Thrace under Antonius Pius. Her relics were translated to the isle of Lemnos, and the Orthodox Church celebrates her feast on September 16.

Mel and Tina are the diminutive forms.

MELPOMENE
(mel.pom.'uh.ne)

(F) In Greek mythology, MELPOMENE is the Muse of Tragedy. Her name signifies "crying out."

Mel is a diminutive.

MEMNON
(mem.'non)

(M) The Orthodox Church observes April 28, in memory of Memnon, the miracle worker.

MENAS
(mḗ.nahs)
MENNAS
(men.́ahs)

(M) MENAS, an Egyptian by birth, was killed in Egypt c. 300, for proclaiming his Christian faith. The Orthodox Church honors his memory on December 10.

MENELAUS
(men.uh.lā.́uhs)

(M) MENELAUS, of Greek legend, is the king of Sparta, husband of Helen, and brother of Agamemnon.

MENOS
(mḗ.nohs)

(M) Variant spelling of MENAS. See MENAS.

MERCEDES
(mer.sed.ḗ) or
(mer.sā.́dēz)

(F) This name is the Spanish shortened form from (Maria de) MERCEDES -- "Mary of Mercies."

MEROPE
(mer.́ōp)

(F) MEROPE, a native of the isle of Chios, made pilgrimages to shrines of martyrs. She was accused of hiding the body of St. Isidore, and admitted that she, indeed, had hid his body. St. MEROPE was severely beaten, and died in prison from the effects of the beating. The Orthodox Church observes her feast on November 23.

MERRILL
(mer.́uhl)

(M) A variant form of MYRON. See MYRON.

MERTA
(mer.́tah)

(F) A variant of MYRTLE. See MYRTLE.

METHODIOS
(meth.́ō.dē.uhs)

(M) St. METHODIOS is remembered in the Orthodox Church on June 14. As Patriarch of Constantinople (847), he fostered the veneration of icons, and was the first to celebrate the feast of Orthodoxy, which is celebrated on the first Sunday of Lent.

METIS
(mē.́tuhs)

(F) The word, from Greek, means "prudence." METIS warned Zeus that if she bore him a child it would be greater than he. There upon, Zeus swalled the child, and later, Athena sprang from his head.

MICAH
(mī.́kah)

(M) This name, from the Hebrew, is translated as "which is like Jehovah." MICAH the Prophet is remembered in the Orthodox Church on August 14.

MICHAEL
(mī.́kuhl)

(M) "Who is like God" is the translation from the Hebrew. MICHAEL is the only angel called an archangel in the Bible. (See Gabriel). Archangel MICHAEL is the guardian of the chosen people, as related in the Book of Daniel. The Feast of Archangel MICHAEL is celebrated on November 8.

The English and the Russian diminutive forms are Mike and Misha, respectively.

MICHAELA
(mik.'el.ah)

(F) The feminine form of MICHAEL. See MICHAEL.

MICHELLE
(mi.shel)

(F) The French feminine form of MICHAEL. See MICHAEL.

MILES
(mīls)

(M) "Millstone" is the Greek meaning of this name. St. MILES is remembered in the Orthodox Church on November 10.

MILO
(mī.'lō)

(M) A variant spelling of MILES. See MILES.

MILTIADES
(mil.tī.'uh.dēz)

(M) MILTIADES is the famous Athenian general who lived c. 540-488? B.C., and was the victor at the Battle of Marathon.

Milt is a diminutive form.

MIMI
(mē.'me)

(M) A Greek pet name for names such as Demetri and Diomedos.

MIRIAM
(mer.'e.ahm)

(F) Some authorities translate this name, from the Hebrew, as "longed for child." It is the earliest form of MARY and it is the Grecized form of the name. MIRIAM, of the Old Testament, is the sister of Moses. In the Christian era, MIRIAM is the sister of the Apostle Philip, and the Orthodox Church observes her feast on February 17.

MODESTA,
MODESTE
(mō.des.'tah),
(mō.dest)

(F) This name is from the Latin meaning "shy; unassuming." The Orthodox Church remembers St. MODESTOS on December 16.

Desta and Deste are the diminutives.

MOIRA
(mor.'ah)

(F) This is the anglicization of the Irish form of Mary-Máire.

MOLLIE, MOLLY
(mol.'ē), (mol.'ē)

(F) Diminutive forms of MARY.

MONICA
(mon.'uh.ka)

(F) The name comes to us from the Late Latin and is probably of African origin. The word means "advisor." There is also evidence that the name stems from Dominica. MONICA is the name of the mother of St. Augustine.

MONIQUE
(mō.nēk)

(F) The French form of MONICA. See MONICA.

MOREL
(mor.'uhl)

(M) A variant form of MAURICE. See MAURICE.

MORGAN
(mor.'guhn)

(M/F) The name MORGAN is from the Latin "morgaso" which is from the Arabic "margan." The Arabic "margan" means "coral," and comes from the Greek "margrites" which means "pearl." See MARGARET.

MORICE
(mor.'ēs)
MORRIS
(mor.'uhs)

(M) Variant spellings of MAURICE. See MAURICE.

MORITZ
(mortz)

(M) German form of MAURICE. See MAURICE.

MOSCHA
(mos.'kah)

(M/F) The name MOSCHA refers to "a sweet smelling plant," in Greek, and in Latin it means "a fly." In addition, MOSCHOS is the second century B.C. bucolic Greek poet. Unfortunately, only a few of his pastorals survive.

MOSES
(mō.'sehs)

(M) This name is, perhaps, an Egyptian word which means "saved rom the water." MOSES is the illustrious prophet and legislator of the Hebrews, who led them from Egypt to the Promised Land, and gave them the Ten Commandments (Exodus 20). The Orthodox Church honors his memory on September 4.

MOURA
(mu.'rah)

(F) The Russian form for MAURA. See MAURA.

MYLES
(mīls)

(M) A variant spelling for MILES. See MILES.

MYRA
(mī.'rah)

(F) "She who weeps or laments" is the meaning of the Greek name.

MYRON
(mī.'rohn)

(M) This masculine name is from the Greek "muron" which means "sweet oil; perfume; something delightful." MYRON, of ancient Greece, is the 5th century B.C. sculptor whose most celebrated work is DISCOBOLUS. There are Christian men named MYRON who died for Christ, and are remembered in the Orthodox Church. St. MYRON the Wonderworker, a bishop of Crete (died c. 350 A.D.), is remembered on August 8. St. MYRON, the priest, boldly faced his persecutors when they came to destroy his church, and was martyred at Cyzicus, which is located on the Sea of Marmora. He died c. 250 A.D.

MYRTLE
(mer'tl)

(F) "A victorious crown" is the translation of this name from the Greek.

N

NADIA
(nā.́de.ah)

(F) This is the Serbian form of the Russian NADEZHDA which means "hope." See HOPE, ELPIS.

NADINE
(nā.dēn)́

(F) NADINE is the French version of the Russian NADEZHDA.
The diminutive form is Nada.

NANA
(nan.́ah)

(F) The Orthodox Church observes the Feast of St. NANA on November 20.

NANCY
(nan.́sē)

(F) NANCY is either a form of Agnes and/or Anna.
See AGNES, ANNA.

NAOMI
(nā.ō.́mē)

(F) From the Hebrew, this name is translated as "pleasant." NAOMI is the mother-in-law of Ruth. The story of Ruth and her mother-in-law is recounted in the Old Testament Book of Ruth.

NARCISSUS
(nar.sis.́uhs)

(F/M) The NARCISSUS, of ancient Greek mythology, is the beautiful youth who fell in love with his own reflection in the pool. When he began to pine away, he was changed into a flower that bears his name. The name appears in the New Testament in Romans 16:11. NARCISSUS is a Roman whose household St. Paul calls "Christians." In addition to NARCISSUS of the New Testament, St. NARCISSUS, the Archbishop of Jerusalem, is commemorated on August 7, in the Orthodox Chruch.

NATALE
(nat.́uh.lē)

(F) Variant form of NATALIA. See NATALIA.

NATALEE
(nat.uh.lē)́

(F) Variant form of NATALIA. See NATALIA.

NATHALIE (nath.'uh.lē)	(F) Variant form of NATALIA. See NATALIA.
NATICA (nat.'uh.ka)	(F) Variant form of NATALIA. See NATALIA.
NATIKA (na.tik.'ah)	(F) Variant form of NATALIA. See NATALIA.

NATALIA,
NATALIE
(na.tal.'ē.ah),
(nat.'uh.lē)

(F) NATALIA is the Latin feminine form from "dies natalis"--"birthday," that is, Christ's birthday--Christmas, and the name NOEL is related to it. The Orthodox Church observes the memory of St. NATALIA on August 26. St. NATALIA is the woman of Nicomedia, who ministered to the imprisoned martyrs during the persecution of Diocletian. She survived the persecution, and died in Constantinople c. 311.

NATALIOS
(na.tal.'ē.ohs)

(M) Masculine form of NATALIA. St. NATALIOS the Righteous is remembered on May 30, in the Orthodox Church.
NAT is a diminutive form of the name.

NATASHA
(na.ta.'shah)

(F) The Russian form of NATALIA. See NATALIA.

NATHAN
(nā.'thahn)

(M) NATHAN is translated as "a gift" from the Hebrew. This name appears a few times in the Old Testament. NATHAN is a prophet and friend of David (II Chronicles 29:25), and again, NATHAN is the son of David, and an ancestor of Jesus (I Chronicles 3:5). NATHAN is memorialized in the Orthodox Church on the Sunday of Our Lord's Progenitors.

NATHANAEL,
NATHANIEL
(nath.an.'uh.ēl)
(nath.an.'yel)

(M) The Hebrew meaning is "gift of God." NATHANIEL, whose alternate name is Bartholomew, is a disciple of Christ (John 21:2). The Orthodox Church observes his feast on April 22.

NAUSECAA,
NAUSICCA
(no.sik.'ā.ah),
(no.sik.'ah)

(F) NAUSECAA is the maiden, in Greek mythology, who befriended the shipwrecked Odysseus. She persuaded her father to be kind to the visitor. Some legends report that NAUSECCA later married Telemachus, Odysseus' son.

NECTARIOS
(nek.tar.'ē.ohs)

(M) The modern day St. NECTARIOS the Righteous is remembered on November 9, in the Orthodox Church.
Nector is the diminutive form.

NEISA, NIS (nē.'sah), (nis) NYSA (nī.'sah)	(M) Variant spellings of NEYSA. See NEYSA. (M) Variant spelling of NEYSA. See NEYSA.
NEKETA (nē.kē.'tah)	(M) Variant form of NICHOLAS. See NICHOLAS.
NEOPHYTUS (neō.fī.'tuhs)	(M) The name NEOPHYTUS neams "newly illuminated." The Orthodox Church observes December 7, January 21, and May 5, in memory of the martyrs NEOPHYTUS who worked in the vineyard of Christ and gave their lives for Him.
NERINE (ner.īn)	(F) This is the name of the sea nymph from Greek mythology.
NESTOR (nes.'tuhr)	(M) The name NESTOR is from the Greek and is translated as "venerable; wisdom." The NESTOR, of ancient Greek legends, was involved in the Trojan war where he distinguished himself by his eloquence, justice, and wisdom. The name NESTOR appears several times in the Orthodox martyrology, and the notable St. NESTOR is the friend of St. Demetrios (see DEMETRIOS). The Orthodox Church commemorates his memory on October 27.
NEYSA (nē.'sah)	(M) "Pure" is the meaning of this Greek name. St. NEYSA is remembered on February 27, in the Orthodox Church.
NICHOL (nīk.'ahl) NICOLA (ni.kō.'lah)	(F) Variant form for the feminine of NICHOLA. See NICHOLAS. (F) Variant form for the feminine of NICHOLA. See NICHOLAS.
NICOLE (ni.kōl) NIHOLA (ni.hō.'lah)	(F) Variant form for the feminine of NICHOLA. See NICHOLAS. (F) Variant form for the feminine of NICHOLA. See NICHOLAS.
NICOLETTE (nik.ō.'let)	(F) Variant form for the feminine of NICHOLA. See NICHOLAS.
NICHOLAS (nik.'ō.lahs)	(M) "Victory for the people" is the translation of this Greek name. Several men named NICHOLAS are honored in the Orthodox Church, but the most revered and celebrated NICHOLAS is St. NICHOLAS, Bishop of Myra of the early 4th century. He is noted for his philanthropic deeds. The

English corruption of the Dutch, St. NICHOLAS ("Sinterklaas") gives us the modern day "Santa Claus." The feast of St. NICHOLAS is celebrated on December 6.

Nick, Nickie, and Cole are some of the diminutives.

NICIAS, NIKIAS
(nĭ.se͞.ahs),
(nĭ.ke͞.ahs)

(M) NIKIAS is the Athenian who was distinguished as a military commander in the Peloponnasian War.

Nick is a diminutive form.

NICO, NIKO
(nĭ.ko͞), (nik.o͞)

(M) This Greek name means "victory."

NICODEMUS
(nik.o͞.de͞.muhs)

(M) "Conqueror of the people" is the possible explanation of this Greek word. The name is found in the New Testament. NICODEMUS is the wealthy follower of Christ, and a member of the Sanhedrin (John 7:50). The Orthodox Church observes his memory on the Sunday of the Myrrh-Bearing women, which is the second Sunday after Easter.

Nick is a diminutive form.

NIKE, NIKI
(nĭ.k͞), (ne͞.ke͞)

(F) NIKI is the Greek winged-goddess of Victory. The famous Greek statute "Winged Victory" is on display at the Louvre, in France.

St. Niki, the martyr, is remembered on April 16, and 25, in the Orthodox Church.

NIKEFOROS
(nĭ.kif.o͞.rohs)

(M) The translation of this name, from the Greek, is "bearer of victory." NIKEFOROS, although a layman, was called upon to be the Patriarch of Constantinople in 806. Because of the political atmosphere, he came into disagreement and was exiled to a monastary on the Bosphorus. The Orthodox Church commemorates his memory on March 13.

A diminutive form is Nick.

NIKON
(nĭ.kuhn)

(M) Nikon is the Roman soldier who became a Christian and a monk while traveling in the East. Several disciples gathered around him, and when the persecution threatened them in Palestine, they fled to Sicily, but they were martyred under Decius c. 250 A.D. The Orthodox Church observes his memory on March 23.

NILES
(nĭlz)

(M) This is the Greek word for the Nile River. St. NILES, a bishop, is honored on September 17, in the Orthodox Church.

NIOBE
(nī'.ō.bē)

(F) NIOBE, in Greek mythology, is the daughter of Tantalus and Dione. NIOBE had several children and taunted Leto for only having two children. The tormented Leto appealed to the gods for revenge and consequently, all of NIOBE's children were killed except Chloris. NIOBE was turned into a stone.

NIPHA
(nī'.fah)

(F) "Snowflake" is the translation of this Greek word.

NITA
(nī'.tah)

(F) The Orthodox Church observes October 28, in memory of St. NITA, martyr.

NITSA
(nē'.tsah)

(F) A Greek diminutive pet name - Helen-Helenitsa; Evangeline-Evangelista.

NOAH
(nō'.a)

(M) In Hebrew, NOAH means "rest; comfort; peace." NOAH is the name of the celebrated patriarch, who with his family, was preserved by God by means of the ark. NOAH is memorialized in the Orthodox Church on the Sunday of Our Lord's Progenitors.

NOMIKI
(nō.mē.kē')

(F) Feminine of NOMIKOS. See NOMIKOS. Mikie is a diminutive.

NOMIKOS
(nom'.ē.kuhs)

(M) "Learned in the law" is the Greek translation, Mikie is a diminutive.

NONA
(nō'.nah)

(F) In Latin, NONA means "the ninth born." St. NONA is the mother of St. Gregory the Theologian, and her memory is observed on August 5.

NORA
(nor'.ah)

(F) NORA is a contraction of HONORIA. See HONORIA.

O

*Holla your name to reverberate hills,
And make the babbling gossip of the air
Cry out, "Olivia!"*
Shakespeare, **Twelfth Night**

OBADIAH
(ō.bah.dī.ah)

(M) The Hebrew meaning of this name is "servant of Jehovah," and the name is translated as ABDIAS in Greek. OBADIAH is one of the Minor Prophets of the OLD TESTAMENT who lived c. sixth century B.C. The Orthodox Church honors him on November 19.

Obie is a diminutive form of the name.

OCEANUS
(ō.sē.ah.nuhs)

(M) The Orthodox Church commemorates the memory of St. Oceanus martyr on September 4.

ODYSSEUS
(ō.dis.uhs) or
(ō.dis.ē.uhs)

(M) The legendary Greek hero ODYSSEUS, the King of Ithaca, who is married to Penelope, and is the father of Telemachus. is the leading hero of the Trojan War. **The Iliad** and **The Odyssey** contain accounts of his accomplishments and misfortunes.

OLETHIA
(ō.leth.ē.ah)

(F) A variant form of ALETHA. See ALETHA.

OLGA
(ol.gah)

(F) This Teutonic word signifies "holy." St. OLGA a 10th century saint, spread the Christian gospel in Russia. OLGA was the wife of the Duke of Kiev, and during a visit to Constantinople, she was baptized. On her return to Russia, she devoted her life to the spreading of Christianity. She worked at this until her death in 968. The Orthodox Church commemorates her memory on July 11.

OLIVIA, OLIVE
(ō.liv.ē.ah), (ol.iv)

(F) "An olive;" perhaps, "olive-complexion" is the Latin implication of this name. In Greek mythology, the olive tree is sacred to Athena as it was her gift to the city in her contest with Poseidon. The olive tree plays an important role in the Old Testament, for it was the olive leaf that

119

the dove held in her beak when she returned to Noah. This olive leaf indicated that the Great Flood was subsiding. (Genesis 8:11).

OLYMPAS
(ō.lim.́puhs)

(M) In the New Testament (Romans 16:15), we learn of a Christian man named OLYMPUS. The Orthodox Church commemorates the memory of St. OLYMPAS, the apostle, on November 10.

OLYMPIA
(ō.limp.́e.ah)

(F) The Greek translation means "heavenly; of the mountain of the gods." Even though the name has its roots in the pagan religion of the ancient Greeks, the name appears in Church history. In the early 5th century, Olympia is a deaconess at Constantinople and a friend of St. John Chrysostom. Because of her loyalty to him, OLYMPIA suffered exile and poverty. OLYMPIA, who belonged to one of the great families of Constantinople, lost both of her parents while very young. She was raised by Theodosia, a relative of St. Basil and St. Gregory of Nazianzus. When she was eighteen she married, but her husband died. The Emperor Theodosius insisted that she remarry, but she refused, and said that if God wanted her to live as a wife, He would not have taken her husband. She was consecrated a deaconess in her early twenties by Archbishop Nectarius, and spent her life working in the vineyard of Christ. She built a convent, and maintained a hospital and an orphanage. The Orthodox commemorates the memory of St. OLYMPIA the Righteous on July 25.

ONESIMUS
(ō.nis.́uh.muhs)

(M) The word ONESIMUS means "profit." We read in Colossian 4:9 that ONESIMUS, a slave to Philemon, ran away and fled to Rome. While there, he was converted to Christianity through Paul's preaching. ONESIMUS was the reason Paul wrote the "Epistle to Philemon." ONESIMUS cared for Paul during Paul's imprisonment. Subsequently, OSENIMUS was received by his former master as "a brother beloved."

Several men named ONESIMUS gave their lives for Christ, and the Orthodox Church observes the days of November 22, December 1, May 10, and Julyl 14, in their memory.

ONESIPHORUS
(ō.nē.sif.́or.uhs)

(M) "Profit bearing" is the meaning of this Greek name. ONESIPHORUS is the Christian friend of

Paul at Ephesus. He went to Rome in search of Paul and found him in prison. Without regard to his own danger, ONESIPHORUS assisted Paul during his imprisonment (II Timothy 1:16-18; 4:19). The Orthodox commemorates his memory on September 7.

ONUPHRIUS
(on.u.frḛ.́uhs)

(M) ONUPHRIUS is the Egyptian who lived as a hermit for seventy years in the desert of Thebias, in Upper Egypt. The Orthodox Church observes his feast on June 12.

Some authorities suggest that the English equivalent of ONUPHRIUS is HUMPHREY.

OPHELIA
(ō.fe.́lḛ.ah)

(F) The meaning of name OPHELIA is "help." Some suggest that the name has its roots in "ophis" which means "serpent" in Greek.

Phelia is a diminutive form.

ORESTES
(o.res.́tēz)

(M) In Greek mythology, ORESTES is the son of Agamemnon, and slayer of his mother Clytemnestra. Christianity also gives us an ORESTES, and the Orthodox Church observes his memory on November 10.

ORETHA
(ō.rḛ.́thah)

(F) In ancient Arcadia and Laconia of Greece, Artemis was referred to as ORETHA.

OTIS
(ō.́tihs)

(M) In Greek, the word means "keen-eared."

-OULA
(ōō.́lah)

(F) A Greek diminutive feminine suffix is affixed to names such as Panagiota becomes Panagiotoula. The preceeding consonant is attached to the suffix and the name becomes Toula.

OURANIA
(ōō.rā.ne.ah)

(F) A variant spelling of URANIA. See URANIA.

OWEN
(ō.́wen)

(M) This name is the Welsh form of the Greek EUGENTIUS. See EUGENE.

OWENA
(o.wḛ.́nah)

(F) Feminine form of OWEN. See OWEN.

P

*I Understand the fury in your words,
but not the words.*
Shakespeare, **Othello**

PABLO
(pab.lō)

(M) Spanish form for PAUL. See PAUL.

PAMELA
(pam.ah.la)

(F) The Greek definition of this name is "all honey."

PANAGIOTA
(pan.ah.gē.ō.tah)

(F) "All holy" is the Greek meaning of this name and the Theotokos is referred to as Panaghia. The Greeks name their daughters in honor of the Theotokos and these girls are called Panagiota. The name, in America, has been brutishly mistranslated as Bertha, Peggy, Pat, Portia, and so on. The Italian name MADONNA, which refers to the Blessed Virgin, is a more proper translation; however, MARIAN or any of the derivatives of MARIA are proper and may be used for the English equivalent. The Orthodox Church celebrates several days throughout the year in honor of the Theotokos. See MARIA.

PANAGIOTES
(pan.ah.gē.ō.tuhs)

(M) This is the masculine of PANAGIOTA. See PANAGIOTA. This name too, has suffered mistranslation as boys, who are christened PANAGIOTES, are often called PETER. A truer equivalent for the name PANAGIOTES is Mario or Marion. In addition to the feast days which are observed for PANAGIOTA, June 24, is observed in memory of the neomartyr, St. PANAGIOTES, in the Orthodox Church.
Panos is a diminutive form.

PANTELEMON
(pan.tel.ē.mon)

(M) The meaning of this Greek name is "all-merciful; all-compassionate." St. PANTELEMON is the doctor and martyr, who was born in 275 A.D., at Asia Minor. As a skilled physician, his reputation was known throughout

122

the empire. His acquaintance with the devoted Christian, Ermolaos, led to his conversion to Christianity. He continued his work as a physician, and worked many miracles in the name of Jesus Christ. Emperor Maximinian heard of these feats and ordered PANTELEMON to give up his new faith and return to the pagan gods. PANTELEMON refused, and suffered martyrdom on July 27, 304 A.D. The Orthodox Church commemorates his memory on July 27.

Diminutive forms include Panteli, Leon and Telly.

PANTELEMONOS
(pan.te.lḗ.mon.uhs.)
(M) Variant spelling of PANTELEMON. See PANTELEMON.

PANTELEIMON
(pan.te.lḗ.mon)
(M) Variant spelling of PANTELEMON. See PANTELEMON.

PANTALEON
(pan.tah.lḗ.ohn)
(M) Variant spelling of PANTELEMON. See PANTELEMON.

PANTILEON
(pan.ti.lḗ.on)
(M) Variant spelling of PANTELEMON. See PANTELEMON.

PARASCEVE
PARASKEVE
(pa.ra.ske.vē),
(pa.ra.ské.vē)
(F) In ancient Greek, the word means "preparing, a getting ready." It now means "getting ready for the Sabbath." The Orthodox Church commemorates the memory of St. PARASKEVE the Righteous martyr on July 26. See PETKA.

PARASKEVAS,
PARASKEVES
(pa.raś.ke.vahs)
(pa.ras.kēvź)
(M) Masculine form of Paraskeve. The Orthodox Church observes the memory of St. PARASKEVAS on Marcy 1.

A diminutive form is Skevas.

PARMENAS
(par.meń.uhs)
(M) "Abiding" is the translation of this name from the Greek. PARMENAS is one of the first seven deacons chosen by the Apostles to help in their work (Acts 6:5). His memory is observed on July 28, in the Orthodox Church.

A diminutive form is Menas.

PARNELL
(par.neĺ)
(M) A variant form of PETER. See PETER.

PARTHEN
(par.́then)
(F) Variant form of PARTHENA. See PARTHENA.

PARTHINIA
(par.thin.̄e.ah)
(F) Variant form of PARTHENA. See PARTHENA.

PARTHENA
(par.thē´.nah)

(F) This is the Greek word for "sweet virgin." St. PARTHENA is memorialized on January 8, in the Orthodox Church.

PARTHENOS
(par´.then.uhs)

(M) The masculine form of PARTHENA. The Orthodox Church observes February 7, and March 24, in memory of St. PARTHENOS.

PASCAL
(pas´.kahl)

(M) The English equivalent of LAMBROS. See LAMBROS.

PATRICE
(pa.trēs´)

(F) French feminine form of PATRICIA. See PATRICIA.

PATRICIA
(pa.tri´.shah)

(F) Feminine of PATRICK. See PATRICK. The Orthodox Church observes the memory of St. PATRICIA, the martyr, on August 9.

Diminutive forms are Pat, Patsy, Patty and Kiki.

PATRICK
(pat´.rik)

(M) "Noble, patrician" is the Latin meaning of this name. The Orthodox Church remembers St. PATRICK, the martyr, on May 19.

Pat is a diminutive form.

PAUL
(paul)

(M) The Latin meaning of this name implies "little." St. Paul, the distinguished apostle of the Gentiles (Romans 11:13), was originally named Saul, but he changed his name to PAUL in honor of Sergius Paulus, whom he converted (Acts 13: 16-12). St. PAUL traveled to many regions, converted many people, founded numerous churches, endured many trials, performed miracles, wrote many epistles, and died a martyr's death. St PAUL was beheaded in Rome, on the same day St. PETER was crucified, head downward. The Orthodox Church honors the memory of St. PAUL on June 29.

PAULA
(paul´.ah)

(F) Feminine form of PAUL. See PAUL. Girls christened with the name PAULA commemorate the Feast of St. PAUL on June 29; however, a St. PAULA suffered martyrdom, and the Orthodox Church observes her memory on June 3.

PAULINA
(paul´.ē.nah)

(F) Feminine variant of PAUL. See PAUL.

PAULINE
(paul.lēn´)

(F) Feminine variant of PAUL. See PAUL.

PAVEL
(pa.vel´)

(M) The Russian form of PAUL. See PAUL.

124

PEARCE (pers)	(M) A variant form of PETER. See PETER.
PEARL, PEARLE (perl), (perl)	(F) English equivalent of MARGARET. See MARGARET.
PERL, PERLE (perl), (perl)	(F) English equivalent of MARGARET. See MARGARET.
PEDRO (pā.dro͞)	(M) Spanish form of PETER. See PETER.
PELAGA, PELAGI, PELAGIA (pe.lagah), (pe.laj.e͞.ah)	(F) "Woman of sorrows" is the Latin translation for this name. St. PELAGIA, a maid of Tarsus, is said to have been roasted to death for refusing to marry a son of Diocletian. The Orthodox Church observes the memory of St. PELAGIA the Righteous on May 4. Pele is a diminutive form.
PENELOPE (pe.nel.o͞.pe͞)	(F) This name in Greek means "weaver." PENELOPE, of Greek legend, is the wife of Odysseus and the mother of Telemachos. She is the faithful wife who put off would-be suitors by weaving a coat by day for her father-in-law, and undoing her work at night. She is the model of domestic virtue. Diminutive forms include Penny and Poppy.
PERICLES (per.ah.kle͞z)	(M) PERICLES is the Greek statesman whose age was the most flourishing period of Grecian art and science. He was born c. 498 B.C., and died c. 429 B.C. Perry is a diminutive form.
PERNELL (per.nel)	(M) A variant form of PETER. See PETER.
PERPETUA (per.pet.u͞.ah)	(F) This Latin word connotes "everlasting." February 1, is observed in memory of St. Perpetua, the martyr, in the Orthodox Church. Petta is a diminutive form of the name.
PERRIN (per.in)	(M) Variant form of PETER. See PETER.
PERSEPHONE (per.sef.o͞.ne͞)	(F) In Greek mythology, PERESOPHONE is the daughter of Zeus and Demeter, who was abducted by Hades. Since she ate seven pomgranate seeds while she was with Hades, PERSEPHONE was required to remain with him for seven months of the year, and could return to her mother for the other five months. Thus, the ancient Greeks explained the change of the seasons.

PERSIS
(per.'sihs)

(F) This Greek name can be translated either as "a girl of peace" or "a Persian woman." In Romans 16:17, PERSIS is a Christian lady in Rome whom St. PAUL refers to as "the beloved." The Orthodox Church commemorates the memory of St. PERSIS, the martyr, on September 24.

PETER
(pē.'tehr)

(M) "Rock or stone" is the meaning of this Greek name. St. PETER, whose Aramaic name is Cephas and means "rock", was translated into Greek as "petra." St. PETER is one of the Twelve Apostles. It appears that he left a good business and a comfortable home to follow Christ (Mark 10:28). St. PETER was the spokesman of the Apostles on the day of Pentecost and the Death and Resurrection of Christ led to a change in this Apostle. He became bold and steadfast in his mission, which eventually led to giving his life for Christ. He was crucified, head down (at his request) in Rome on the same day St. Paul was beheaded. The Orthodox Church memorializes St. PETER on June 29.
Pete, Petey, Petie are diminutive forms.

PETKA
(pet.'kah)

(F) The Serbian form of PARASKEVE. See PARASKEVE.

PETRA
(pet.'rah)

(F) A feminine form of PETER. See PETER.

PETRIE
(pet.'rē)

(M) A variant form of PETER. See PETER.

PETRINA
(pe.trē.'nah)

(F) Feminine variant form of PETER. See PETER.

PETRINE
(pe.trēn)́

(F) Feminine variant form of PETER. See PETER.

PETRONELLA,
PETRONILLA
(pe.trō.nel.'ah)
(pe.trō.nil.'ah)

(F) Feminine form of PETER. The Orthodox Church observes May 31, in memory of St. PETRONELLA.
Peti and Petie are diminutive forms.

PETRONIA
(pe.tro.nē.'ah)

(F) Feminine form of PETER. The memory of St. PETRONIA is observed on September 29, in the Orthodox Church.
Diminutive forms are Peti and Petie.

PHAEDRA
(fē.'dra)

(F) In classical mythology, PHAEDRA is the daughter of Minos, and is the second wife of Theseus. She was enamored with her stepson,

Hippolytus, who did not share those feelings. Enraged, she hanged herself, but left a note accusing him of a criminal attempt on her honor. Theseus, in his anger, cursed his son and Hippolytus met with a tragic death. Later, Theseus learned the truth that Hippolytus was innocent.

In the annals of Church history, St. PHAEDRA, martyr, is remembered on November 29, and April 21 in the Orthodox Church.

PHEBE
(fē.bē)

(F) A variant spelling for PHOEBE. See PHOEBE.

PHELE
(fē.lē)

(M) A variant spelling for PHILO. See PHILO.

PHELPS
(felps)

(M) A variant spelling of PHILIP. See PHILIP.

PHENICE
(fē.nis)

(F) PHENICE is from the Hebrew and means "from a palm tree."

PHILANA
(fil.an.ah)

(F) PHILANA is from the Greek and means "friend of mankind."

PHILANDER
(fil.and.ehr)

(M) "Man who loves mankind," is the interpetation of this Greek word.

Diminutives include Philan and Phil.

PHILARETOS
(fil.ah.rē.tos)

(M) "Friend of good" is the Greek meaning of this word. St. PHILARETOS is remembered for his many philanthropic deeds, and the Orthodox Church commemorates his memory on December 1.

Phil is a diminutive form.

PHILEMON
(fil.eh.mon)

(M) The name PHILEMON means "a man of great beauty," in Greek. PHILEMON and his wife, of Greek mythology, were the poor cottagers who entertained Zeus and Apollo. They were disguised as travelers, and the hospitality of this poor couple so impressed Zeus that he transformed their humble cottage into a temple. Zeus also granted them their wish that they might die together.

Moreover, the name PHILEMON appears in the New Testament. St. PHILEMON is the wealthy resident of Colossae, and a man of great influence, who was converted to Christianity by St. Paul. When St. Paul was near the close of his first imprisonment at Rome (62-63 A.D.), he wrote to PHILEMON and thus, it is, that we have

the New Testament book, The Epistle to
Philemon. The Orthodox Church observes the
memory of St. PHILEMON the apostle on
November 22.

PHILIP, PHILLIP
(fil.'uhp), (fil.'uhp)

(M) The Greek meaning of PHILIP is "a lover of
horses." Ancient Greek history boasts of PHILIP
of Macedon, the bold and warlike ruler, who was
the father of Alexander the Great. Nevertheless,
the name appears proudly in the annals of Christianity for St. PHILIP is the fourth of the twelve
apostles chosen by Jesus Christ. PHILIP is the only Apostle who had a Greek name and probably
spoke Greek, since it was to him who "certain
Greeks" came to request to be admitted to see
Jesus (John 12:20-22). The Orthodox observes his
feast on November 14.

Again, the name PHILIP appears in the New
Testament as PHILIP, the deacon. PHILIP was
with Stephen and five others, all Greeks, who were
chosen by the Apostles to administer the economic
affairs of the Church in Jerusalem (Acts 6). The
Orthodox Church observes his feast on October
11.

The diminutive form is Phil.

PHILIPPA
(fil.ip.'ah)

(F) Feminine form of PHILIP. See PHILIP. St.
PHILIPPA is the mother of St. Theodore, and
her memory is observed on April 19, in the Orthodox Church.

PHILLIDA
(fi.li.'dah)

(F) "Loving woman" is the Greek meaning of this
name.

PHILO
(fi.'lo)

(M) "Love" is the meaning of this Greek name.
The Orthodox Church memorializes St. PHILO,
bishop on January 24.

PHILOLOGUS
(fi.lo.'lo.juhs)

(M) The name PHILOLOGUS means "lover of
letters" in Greek. St. PHILOLOGUS is the Chris-
tian at Rome whom St. Paul salutes in Paul's
Epistle to the Romans 16:15. The Orthodox
Church commemorates the memory of St.
PHILOLOGUS, the apostle, on November 5.

Philo is a diminutive form.

PHILOMELA
(fil.uh.ma.'lah)

(F) "Friendly speech" is the meaning of this
Greek name. PHILOMELA, of ancient Greece, is
the daughter of Pandion, King of Athens. After
being raped and having her tongue cut out by
Tereus, she was turned into either a nightingale or

a swallow.

PHILOMENA
(fil.ō.mē´.nah)

(F) Feminine form of PHILOMENOS. See PHILOMENOS.

PHILOMENOS
(fī.lō´.men.ohs)

(M) This Greek name means "loving friend." November 29, is observed in honor of St. PHILOMENOS, martyr, in the Orthodox Church.

PHILOTHEA
(fil.ō´.thē.ah)

(F) "One who loves God" is the Greek meaning of this name. St. PHILOTHEA, of Athens, lived in the 16th century, and is remembered for her philanthropy. She became a widow at a very early age, probably at sixteen. She, subsequently, became a nun in the Orthodox Church and founded convents. These convents, not only provided for the spiritual environment, but allowed the women to do weaving and other handcraft for the benefit of the poor. The Orthodox Church honors her memory on February 19.

Diminutives include Philo and Thea.

PHILOTHEOS
(fil.ō´.the.ohs)

(M) Masculine form of PHILOTHEA. See PHILOTHEA. The Orthodox Church observes the memory of St. PHILOTHEOS, martyr, on January 29.

Phil and Philo are diminutive forms.

PHINEAS
(fin´.e.ahs)

(M) In Hebrew, PHINEAS means "mouth of brass." The Book of Exodus 6:25, reveals that PHINEAS is the son of Eleazer and the grandson of Aaron. The Orthodox Church honors PHINEAS on September 2.

PHOCAS
(fō´.kahs)

(M) St. PHOCAS of Sinope is remembered in Orthodox Church on September 22. He converted many to Christianity, performed many miracles, and was consecrated bishop. During the persecutions of Trojan, he was scalded to death by pagan Roman soldiers.

PHOEBE
(fē´.bē)

(F) "Pure, radiant" is the translation of this Greek word. In Greek mythology, the name PHOEBE appears several times. It is another name for Artemis, the moon goddess; she is one of the first twelve Titans; Phoebe is the daughter of Leucippus; and PHOEBE is the sister of Castor and Pollux. Even though mythology uses the name, PHOEBE is a leading Christian woman in the Church at Cenchreae, a port of ancient Corinth. In Romans 16:1, she is referred to as

"PHOEBE our sister." The Orthodox Church observes September 3, for the feast of St. PHOEBE, the deaconess.

PHOTINA
(fō.'tē.'nah)

(F) "The enlightened one" is the Greek translation of this name. St. PHOTINA is the "woman at the well" who was exiled from her native Samaria, and is known as the Samaritan woman (John 4:5-42). She was baptized by the Apostles, and given the name PHOTINA. With her family, she traveled far to spread Christ's message. PHOTINA and her family were imprisoned in Rome because she spoke for the cause of Christianity before Nero. After two years in prison, they were put to death. The Orthodox Church commemorates her memory on February 26, and on the Sunday of the Samaritan.

Fina and Tina are diminutive forms.

PHOTIUS
(fō.'shuhs)

(M) The Greek meaning of PHOTIUS is "enlightened." The Orthodox Church refers to Epiphany as "Ta Phota - The Light," so, many who are named PHOTIUS celebrate their name day on the Feast of Epiphany, that is, on January 6. St. PHOTIUS, patriarch of Constantinople, is commemorated on February 6, in the Orthodox Church.

Foti and Photi are diminutive forms.

PHYLLIS
(fil.'ihs)

(F) "A green bough" is the translation of this Greek name. The name appears in Greek legend, and PHYLLIS is the daughter of Lycurgus. She fell in love with Demophon, who stopped in Thrace on his way home from the Trojan War. They married and he became king. Soon after, Demophan left for Athens and after-a-while, when he failed to return, PHYLLIS threw herself into the sea.

PIERCE
(pērs)

(M) A variant form of PETER. See PETER.

PIERRE
(pē.ar)

(M) The French form of PETER. See PETER.

PIETRO
(pē.et.'rō)

(M) The Italian form of PETER. See PETER.

PLATO
(plā́:tō)

(M) The word PLATO means "broad" in Greek. No doubt, when one hears the name PLATO, one immediately thinks of PLATO, the great Athenian philosopher, who was a pupil of Socrates and founder of the Academy. PLATO was, originally, named Aristocles, but was called PLATO by his gymnastic teacher, either for his broad shoulders or for the breadth of his forehead.

Nevertheless, our attention can be directed to those Christians named PLATO who died for Christ. PLATO, of the early 9th century, lived in Constantinople. He was orphaned at 13, and was reared by his uncle, who was the imperial treasurer. At the age of 24, PLATO abandoned his estates, which he divided among his sisters, and entered a religious life. He was successful as a monk and as an administrator. When offered a bishopric, he refused it, and even refused to be ordained a priest. However, he became involved in opposing the imperial misdoings of Emperor Constantine Porphyrogentius. PLATO was exiled, mistreated, and finally, released in 811, by Michael I. PLATO spent the remainder of his life bedridden, and in retirement. He died on April 4, 814. The Orthodox observes his memory on April 4.

POLYCARP
(pol:ē.karp)

(M) The Greek meaning is "fruitfulness." St. POLYCARP was convereted by St. John the Evangelist c. 80 A.D., and became bishop of Smyrna c. 96 A.D. He and his friend, St. Ignatius of Antioch, were the link between the Apostles and the Christians in Asia Minor. His devotion to Christ led to his martyrdom, as he was burned alive, along with twelve members of his church. The Orthodox Chuirch observes his memory of February 23.

Ephriam is the Hebrew equivalent of POLYCARP.

POLYCHRONUS
(pol.ē.krō:nuhs)

(M) "Many years" is the translation of this Greek name. The Orthodox Church observes October 7, and February 23, in memory of those named POLYCHRONUS, who suffered a martyr's death for their love of Christ.

Diminutives include Chronos and Ronnie.

POLYDORE,
POLIDORO
(pol.ē.dōr),
(po.lē.dor.'ō)

(M) "With very rich gifts; well-endowed," is the Greek meaning of this name. In Greek legend, POLYDORE is a king of Sparta. The Orthodox Church commemorates the memory of St. POLIDORE, the neomartyr (1794), on September 3.

POLYHYMIA
(pol.ē.him.'ē.ah)

(F) In Greek mythology, POLYHYMIA is the Muse Lyric poetry.

POLYXENE,
POLYXENIA
(pō.lik.'se.nē)
(pō.lik.'se.nē.ah)

(F) The translation of this Greek name is either "very hospitable" or "very foreign." The Orthodox Church observes the memory of POLYXENE, the martyr, on September 23.

Diminutive forms include Polly, Kene, and Xenia.

PRISCILLA
(pri.sil.'ah)

(F) The name PRISCILLA has its roots in the Latin "priscus" which means "ancient." PRISCILLA is a convert of the 1st century, and is the wife of Aquila. Her hospitality and Biblical teachings to Apollos, and her wise counsel to the young Timothy show the value and usefulness of a good mother. (Acts 18; Romans 16; I Corinthians 16:19; and II Tomothy 4:19). The Orthodox Church commemorates her memory on February 13.

PROCOPIOS
(pro.kō.'pē.uhs)

(M) In the 8th century, PROCOPIOS and Basil were two courageous defenders of the venerationof icons against Emperor Leo the Isaurian. The Orthodox Church honors his memory on February 27.

PRODOMOS
(prō.'drō.mohs)

(M) His name in Greek means "forerunner" and refers to St. John the Forerunner. Many boys are named PRODROMOS in honor of St. John.

R

Sweetes' li'l feller--
Everybody knows;
Dunno what ter call 'em,
But he's mighty lak' a rose!
--Stanton "Mighty Lak' a Rose"

RACHEL
(ra̅.chehl)

(F) In Hebrew, this name means "a ewe, lamb." RACHEL, of the Old Testament, is Jacob's chosen and best beloved wife, and the mother of Joseph and Benjamin (Genesis 29:17). The Orthodox Church honors RACHEL on the Sunday of Our Lord's Progenitors.

Rae, Ray, and Shelley are among the diminutive forms.

RACHELLE
(ra.shel)

(F) Variant spelling of RACHEL. See RACHEL.

ROCHELLE
(ro̅.shel)

(F) Variant spelling of RACHEL. See RACHEL.

RAPHEAL
(ra̅.fe̅.uhl)

(M) "Divine healer" is the translation of this Hebrew name. RAPHAEL, one of the archangels, along with Michael, Gabriel and Uriel, stands around the throne of God. RAPHAEL is mentioned in Tobit 12:15, and is remembered in the Orthodox Church on November 8. In addition to this date the Orthdox Church commemorates the memory of St. RAPHAEL on April 9.

RAPHAELA
(ra.fa̅.el.ah)

(F) Feminine of RAPHAEL. See RAPHAEL.

RAQUEL
(ra.kehl)

(F) The Spanish form of RACHEL. See RACHEL.

REBECCA
(re.bek.ah)

(F) The name, in Hebrew, signifies "captivation; a noose cord." REBECCA, of the Old Testament, was so named because of her captivating beauty (Genesis 26:7). REBECCA is the wife of the patriarch Isaac, and the mother of Jacob and

Esau. Her memory is honored on the Sunday of Our Lord's Progenitors in the Orthodox Church.

Some of the diminutive forms of this name are Reba, Riba, Riva, and Becky.

REBEKAH
(re.bek′a)

(F) A variant spelling of REBECCA. See REBECCA.

REGAN
(rē′gahn)

(F) A variant form of REGINA. See REGINA.

REGINA
(re.jē′nah)

(F) The name REGINA is from the Latin, and means "queenly" and is the feminine form of REGINOS. See REGINOS.

As has been previously noted, the name REGINA may be used as the English equivalent of Basiliki or Vasiliki.

Diminutive forms of REGINA are Gina, Reggie, and Rena.

REGINOS
(re.jin′ohs)

(M) "King" is the translation of this name. The Orthodox Church observes February 25, for the feast of St. REGINOS, bishop.

REUBEN
(roō′bin)

(M) "Behold a son" is the Hebrew meaning. REUBEN is the oldest son of Jacob and Leah (Genesis 29:22). His memory is commemorated on the Sunday of Our Lord's Progenitors.

Rube is a diminutive form.

REX
(reks)

(M) The translation of this name, from the Latin, is "king." Rex is the English equivalent for REGINOS and BASIL.

RHODA
(rō′dah)

(F) RHODA is Greek for "a rose." In Acts 12:13-15, RHODA is the maid in the household of Mary, mother of John Mark, and it was RHODA who answered the door to Peter, after he had escaped from prison. St. RHODA is remembered in the Orthodox Church on June 9.

RITA
(rē′tah)

(F) Diminutive form of MARGARITA. See MARGARET.

ROMA
(rō′ma)

(F) "A wanderer" or "a woman of Rome" is the Latin meaning of this name. See ROMAN.

ROMAIN
(rō.mān′)

(M) A variant spelling of ROMAN. See ROMAN.

ROMAN
(rō′man)

(M) The name is from the Latin, and is translated as "of Rome." The Orthodox Church remembers St. ROMAN, the hymnographer, on October 1.

He was a Syrian Jew, who became a priest at Constantinople and the greatest of Greek hymnographers.

ROSA, ROSALEE (F) Variant forms of RHODA.
(rṓ.sah), (rṓ.sah.lē)

ROSALEEN (F) Variant form of RHODA.
(rṓ.sa.lēn)

ROSALIA (F) Variant form of RHODA.
(rō.sal.ḗ.ah)

ROSALIE (F) Variant form of RHODA.
(rṓ.sah.lē)

ROSELLA (F) Variant form of RHODA.
(rō.seĺ.ah)

ROSAMOND (F) Variant form of RHODA.
(rṓ.sah.mond)

ROSENA (F) Variant form of RHODA.
(rṓ.sē.nah)
ROSENE (F) Variant form of RHODA.
(rṓ.sēn)

ROSINA (F) Variant form of RHODA.
(rṓ.sin.ah)
ROSETTA (F) Variant form of RHODA.
(rō.set́.ah)

ROSETTE (F) Variant form of RHODA.
(rō.set́)

ROSABEL (F) "A fair rose" is the translation of this name
(rṓ.sah.behl) from Latin. See RHODA.

ROSALIND (F) Spanish form of RHODA. The name
(rṓ.sah.lind) ROSALIND refers to "a pretty rose." See
RHODA.

ROXANA (F) This name is from the Persian and means
(rokś.an.ah) "dawn of day." SEE AURORA.

RUFUS (M) "Red; red-haired" is the meaning of this
(rū́.fuhs) name from Latin. In Romans 16:13, RUFUS is a
Christian man in Rome. The Orthodox Church
observes April 8, April 28, and September 28, in
memory of St. RUFUS.
Rufe is a diminutive form.

RUTH (F) The Hebrew meaning of RUTH is "a beautiful
(ruth) friend." The name RUTH is found in both the

Old and New Testaments. In Book of RUTH, RUTH is a Moabitess, who returned to Judah with her mother-in-law Naomi. Soon after her return to Judah, she married Boaz, a relative of Noami's husband. From this marriage descended David, and through him our Savior Jesus Christ. The Orthodox Church honors RUTH on the Sunday of Our Lord's Progenitors.

S

I hate the man who builds his name
On ruins of another's fame.
--John Gat **The Poet and the Roses**

SABAS
(sa.´bas)

(M) Two celebrated Christian men named SABAS have left their mark in Church history. St. SABAS, of the 6th century, is a monk, scholar, and a spiritual leader. He and St. Euthymios founded a monastic life that was stern, but this harsh life prepared the monks to defend and preserve Christianity. The memory of St. SABAS the Blessed is observed on December 5, in the Orthodox Church.

The 13th century gives St. SABAS, the patron of the Serbs. St. SABAS established the first monastery for the Serbs at Mount Athos-Chilandarion. He was called out of his beloved monastery by the Patriarch of Constantinople to return Serbia and serve his people as their archbishop. St. SABAS served well and eventually, returned to Chilandarion where he died on January 14, 1236. His memory is observed on January 14, in the Orthodox Church.

SACHA
(sa.´shah)

(M) Russian form for ALEXANDER. See ALEXANDER.

SALVADORE
(sal.´va.dor)

(M) Italian for "Savior." SALVADORE is acceptable as the equivalent for SOTERI. See SOTERI.

Sal is a diminutive form.

SALVATORE
(sal.va.tor.´e)

(M) Spanish for "Savior." See SALVADORE.

SAMEAS
(sa.me.´ahs)

(M) The Orthodox Church observes January 8, in honor of St. SAMEAS, the Elamite prophet.

A diminutive is Sam.

SAMPSON
(samp.´sohn)

(M) A variant spelling of SAMSON. See SAMSON.

137

SAMSON
(sam.'suhn)

(M) "The sun's name" is the translation from the Hebrew. In the Old Testament, Judges 15, we read of the Hebrew hero of unusual strength who is remembered for his fearless deeds, moral infirmities, and for his tragic end.

Furthermore, A Christian SAMSON, known as the Glorious Innkeeper and Physician, is a stellar figure in Christian history. St. SAMSON, a native of Rome, is of the lineage of the Emperor Constantine. Instead of leading a princely life, he pledged himself to the service of God and mankind. St. SAMSON earned a reputation as an excellent physician, who turned his family estate into a clinic. Eventually, he traveled to Constantinople. His reputation had preceded him, and he was called upon to care for Justinian who was ill. Through SAMSON's abilities as a physician, Justinian was cured, and as a reward for SAMSON, Justinian established a medical center in Constaninople. The Orthodox Church observes the memory of St. SAMSON on June 27.

Sam is a diminutive form.

SAMUEL
(sam.'ū.el)

(M) This Hebrew name is translated as "heard of God." SAMUEL, the celebrated Hebrew prophet and judge (Acts 3:24; 13:20), was consecrated to God from the time of his birth (I Samuel 3). SAMUEL anointed Saul and later David, and also instituted "the school of the prophet." SAMUEL the Prophet is remembered by the Orthodox Church on August 20.

Diminutive forms are Sam and Sammy.

SAMUELA
(sam.ū.el.'ah)

(F) Feminine form of SAMUEL. See SAMUEL.

SANDRA
(san.'drah)

(F) A diminutive form of ALEXANDRA and/or Cassandra. See ALEXANDRA and CASSANDRA.

SANTIAGO
(san.tē.ag.'ō)

(M) Spanish form for St. JAMES. See JAMES.

SARA, SARENA
(sar.'ah), (sa.rē.'nah)

(F) Variant forms of SARAH. See SARAH.

SARETTA
(sa.ret.'ah)

(F) Variant form of SARAH. See SARAH.

SARITA
(sa.rē.'tah)

(F) Variant form of SARAH. See SARAH.

SARAH
(sar.'ah)

(F) "A princess" is the implication of this Hebrew name. SARAH is the wife of Abraham (Genesis 20:12), who, though advanced in age, became the mother of Isaac. She was a woman of uncommon beauty, a devoted wife, and a sympathizing mother. (Genesis 24:67). The Orthodox Church honors SARAH on the Sunday of Our Lord's Progenitors.

Sadie, Sal, Sallie, and Sally are diminutive forms.

SAVAS
(sa.'vas)

(M) Variant spelling of SABAS.

SEAN
(shawn)

(M) Irish form of JOHN. See JOHN.

SEBASTE,
SEBASTIA
(se.bas.'tē),
(se.bas.'tē.ah)

(F) Feminine of SEBASTIAN. See SEBASTIAN. The Orthodox Church commemorates the memory of St. SEBASTE, the martyr, on October 24.

SEBASTIAN
(se.bas.'ti.ahn)

(M) "Venerable, reverend" is the meaning of this Greek name. See AUGUSTUS. The Orthodox Church observes the memory of St. SEBASTIAN on December 18, and February 26.

SELENA
(se.lē.'nah)
SELENE
(se.lēn)́

(F) SELENA is the Greek for "the moon." The Orthodox Church commemorates the memory of St. SELENA on June 5.

A diminutive form is LENA.

SERAPHIM
(ser.'ah.fim)

(M) SERAPHIM is the Latinized pural form of the Hebrew "seraph" which means "burning ones." The SERAPHIM is the highest of the Nine Choirs of Angels. These beings were beheld by Isaiah in the vision of God (Isaiah 61:7), and their form is represented as human with the addition of six pairs of wings. Two pair of wings cover the face and feet to signify the deepest humility and reverence, and the other pair of wings execute the will of God. The SERAPHIM are memorialized on November 8. In addition, Christian men named SERAPHIM, who achieved sainthood, are remembered on December 4, March 16, and May 6, in the Orthodox Church.

SERAPHINA
(ser.ah.fē.'nah)

(F) Feminine form of SERAPHIM. See SERAPHIM.

SERAPHINE
(ser.ah.fīn)́

(F) Feminine form of SERAPHIM. See SERAPHIM.

SERENA
(ser.e̅.nah)

(F) Feminine of SERENOS. See SERENOS.

SERENOS
(ser.e̅.nohs)

(M) The Latin meaning of this name is "calm, peaceful, serene." The feast of St. SERENOS is celebrated on July 6, in the Orthodox Church.

SERGE
(serj.eh)

(M) A variant spelling of SERGIOS. See SERGIOS.

SERGIOS
(ser.je̅.ohs)

(M) SERGIOS is a Latin gens. Several men named SERGIOS achieved sainthood, and are remembered by the Orthodox Church on November 28, October 7, January 2, and May 13.

SETH
(seth)

(M) "Appointed" is the translation of this name from the Hebrew. SETH or SHETH is the first son of Adam after the death of Abel (Genesis 4:25). His memory is observed by the Orthodox Church on the Sunday of Our Lord's Progenitors.

SEVASTE
(se.vas.te̅)

(F) A variant spelling of SEBASTE. See SEBASTE.

SHARON
(shar.uhn)

(F) SHARON, a Hebrew word, means "from a fertile plain" and in the Old Testament, the name appears in Song of Solomon 2:1, as "rose of SHARON."

SHAWN
(shawn)

(M) Irish form of JOHN. See JOHN.

SHEILA
(she̅.lah)

(F) Irish variant of CELIA. See CELIA.

SHELLY
(shel.e̅)

(F) A diminutive form of RACHEL. See RACHEL.

SIBEL, SIBELL
(sib.ehl), (sib.ehl)

(F) Variant spellings of SIBYL. See SIBYL.

SIBYL
(si̅.bel)

(F) In classical mythology, SIBYL is a prophetess, who prophecized under the inspiration of a god or goddess.

SIDNEY
(sid.ne̅)

(M) The name SIDNEY is the English corruption of the French, St. DENYS. See DIONYSUS.

SILAS
(si̅.lahs)

(M) This name is from the Latin and means "of the forest." The name SILAS is the contraction of the name SILVANUS. SILVANUS, one of the chiefmen of the early Church at Jerusalem, accompanied Paul and Barnabas to Antioch. SILVANUS carried, with him, a decree from the

Council at Jerusalem, which gave instructions concerning the relation of Gentile converts to the Mosaic Law. (Acts 15:22-30). SILVANUS is again mentioned in II Corinthians 1:19, as Paul talks of his labors.

The Orthodox Church commemorates the memory of St. Silvan on October 14, and St. Silas is remembered on July 30.

SILVAN, SYLVAN
(sil.'van), (sĭl.'van)

(M) Variant forms of SILVANUS. See SILAS.

SILVESTER
(sil.ves.'tehr)

(M) "Bred in the country; rustic" is the Latin connotation of the name SILVESTER. St. SILVESTER, the Pope of Rome, whose reign coincided with Emperor Constantine the Great -314-325 A.D., is remembered in the Orthodox Church on January 2, and March 1.

SIMEON
(sim.'ē.on)

(M) In Hebrew, this name means "hearing." SIMEON is the second son of Jacob and Leah, and is one of "the twelve patriarchs of Israel" (Acts 7:8). In addition, SIMEON is the pious man at Jerusalem who is under the influence of the Holy Spirit (Luke 2:21-35). The Holy Spirit revealed to him that he would live to see the Messiah. When Joseph and the Theotokos presented Jesus to the temple, SIMEON took the Child in his arms and gave thanks to God. The Orthodox Church observes this event on February 3.

SIMON
(sī.'mohn)

(M) "Heard" is the implication of this Hebrew name. SIMON is the eleventh chosen of the Twelve Apostles. He is, sometimes, called SIMON Canaanite, but, more generally, he is referred to as SIMON the Zealot (Luke 6:15). SIMON was a member of the faction known as the "Zealots, who were fierce defenders of Mosaic Law and tradition. His memory is honored in the Orthodox Church on May 10.

SIMONE
(si.'mōn)

(F) Feminine form of SIMON. See SIMON.

SIMONETTE
(sī.muh.net)́

(F) Feminine form of SIMON. See SIMON.

SIMONIDES
(sī.mo.nī.'dēz)

(M) SIMONIDES (c. 556-468 ? B.C.) is the Greek lyric poet who ws a rival of Pindar at Syracuse. He wrote masterful verse in epigrammatic manner, and two of his finest epitaphs are on Marathon

and Thermopylae.
A diminutive is Simon.

SIMPSON (simp.'sohn)	(M) Variant form of SAMSON. See SAMSON.
SIMSON (sim.'suhn)	(M) Variant form of SAMSON. See SAMSON.
SMARAGDA (sma.rag.'dah)	(F) The feminine form of SMARAGDOS. See SMARAGDOS. The English equivalent is "Emerald."
SMARAGDOS (sma.rag.'dohs)	(M) See SMARAGDA. St. SMARAGDOS suffered martyrdom, along with twenty-three others in Rome, under the rule of Diocletian. The Orthodox Church commemorates his memory on March 9.
SOCRATES (sok.'ra.tēs)	(M) SOCRATES is the great Greek philosopher of Athens c. 470-399 B.C. He was the teacher of Plato and was the first to teach "the proper study of mankind is man." SOCRATES was condemned to death for he was found guilty of corrupting the youth by introducing them to new gods. This was impiety. He accepted his death sentence, and drank the hemlock in prison in the presence of his friends. Church history also has several Christian men named SOCRATES who achieved sainthood, and their memory is observed on October 21, November 28, April 10, and April 19.
SOFIA (sō.fī.'ah)	(F) A variant spelling of SOPHIA. See SOPHIA.
SOLON (sō.'lon)	(M) SOLON is one of the Seven Wise Men of Ancient Greece. He is noted for being one of the most cultivated and wisest law givers of all times. As archon in 594 B.C., he moved to protect the peasants of Attica from losing their farms to capitalists; threw open the assembly to all freemen; gave the Areopagus new powers; and he created a new Council of Four Hundred. His goal was a moderate democracy.
SONDRA (son.'drah)	(F) Diminutive form of ALEXANDRA. See ALEXANDRA.
SONIA, SONYA (son.'ē.ah), (son.'yah)	(F) Russian form of SOPHIA. See SOPHIA.
SONJA (son.'yah)	(F) Scandinavian form of SOPHIA. See SOPHIA.

SOPHIA
(so.fē:ah)

(F) The name SOPHIA is from the Greek word "sophos" which means "wisdom". Several saints bear this name, but the most celebrated is St. SOPHIA and her daughters Faith, Hope, and Love. St. SOPHIA and her virgin daughters, ages twelve, ten and nine, suffered martyrdom in Rome under the Emperor Hadrian. The Orthodox Church commemorates their memory on September 17.

It must be noted here, that the great Church of St. SOPHIA (Hagia Sophia), sponsored by Justinian and designed by Athemius of Tralles and Isidorus of Miletus in the 6th century, was not named for the celebrated St. SOPHIA, but was named for that part of the Holy Trinity -- Holy Wisdom.

SOPHIE, SOPHEY
(sō:fē), (sō.fāy)

(F) Variant spellings of SOPHIA. See SOPHIA.

SOPHI, SOPHY
(sō:fe), (sō.fē)

(F) Variant spellings of SOPHIA. See SOPHIA.

SOPHONIAS
(sō.fō.nī:ahs)

(M) The Greek form of ZEPHANIAH. See ZEPHANIAH.

SOPHRONIA
(sō.frō:nē.ah)

(F) "Prudence; common sense" is the Greek meaning. SOPHRONIA is the feminine form of SOPHRONIOS. See SOPHRONIOS.

SOPHRONIOS
(sō.frō:nē.ahs)

(M) "Masculine form of SOPHRONIA." St. SOPHRONIOS is the Syrian who became patriarch of Jerusalem in 633. He spent his life condemming monotheism. The Orthodox Church observes his memory on March 11.

SOPHUS
(sō:fuhs)

(M) Masculine form of SOPHIA. See SOPHIA.

SOTERIA
(so.ter:ē.ah)

(F) The name SOTERIA is from the Greek "soter-savior." In Greek mythology, SOTERIA is another name for Athena. However, this name (which is the feminine of SOTERIOS) refers to the Transfiguration of Our Lord, and is solemnized on August 6 in the Orthodox Church.

In addition to this feast, February 10 is observed in memory of St. SOTERIA, the virgin-martyr. As a young girl under the rule of Decius, she was arrested and tortured for her Christian faith. She survived the torture, but fifty years later suffered death under Diocletian.

A diminutive form is Terry.

SOTERIOS (sō.ter.e.ahs)	(M) This is the masculine form of SOTERIA. See SOTERIA. The appropriate English equivalent is SALVADORE. See SALVADORE. A diminutive form of SOTERIOS is Terry.
SPYRIDON (spī.rid.uhn)	(M) St. SPYRIDON, known as the "Shepherd Bishop," lived in the 4th century. He was born in Cyprus, and as a young boy was a shepherd, who had no formal education. He could not read, but he memorized the Bible by listening to it being read in Church. Because of his piety, SPYRIDON was ordained a priest, elevated to a bishop, and in 325 A.D., he was invited to attend the first Ecumenical Council at Nicaea where he defended Orthodoxy. In his work for Christ, he was persecuted by the Roman soldiers. From the torture he suffered, SPYRIDON lost his right eye. His well preserved body is at the island of Corfu, and his memory is honored on December 12, in the Orthodox Church. Spyro and Spero are diminutive forms of the name.
SPYRIDOULA (spē.rē.dou.lah)	(F) The feminine of SPYRIDON. See SPYRIDON. A diminutive form is Doula.
STACEY, STACY (stā.sē), (stā.sē)	(F) A diminutive form of ANASTASIA. See ANASTASIA.
STAMATINA (sta.ma.tē.nah)	(F) Feminine forms of STAMATIOS. See STAMATIOS. Tami and Tina are diminutive forms.
STAMATIOS (sta.ma.tē.uhs)	(M) The Orthodox Church observes the memory of St. STAMATIOS on August 16.
STAVROS (stav.rohs)	(M) This name from Greek means "cross" and refers to the Cross of Christ's Crucifixion. There is no comparable name in English for a translation, therefore, it is suggested that the name be used in its Greek form. The Orthodox Church observes the feast of the Elevation of the Holy Cross on September 14. Those named STARVOS celebrate their name day on September 14.
STAVROULA (stav.rou.lah)	(F) Feminine form of STAVROS. See STAVROS. Roula is a diminutive form.
STEFAN (stef.ahn)	(M) A variant spelling of STEPHEN. See STEPHEN.

STEFANIE (stef.'an.ē)	(F) A variant spelling of STEPHANIE. See STEPHANIE.
STEFANO (ste.fan.'ō)	(M) Italian form of STEPHEN.
STELIAN (stē.'lē.ahn)	(M) A variant spelling of STYLIAN. See STYLIAN.
STELIANE (stel.'ē.an)	(F) A variant spelling of the feminine form of STYLIAN. See STYLIAN.
STEPHAN, STEVEN (ste.'fahn), (stē.'vehn)	(M) "A crown or garland" is the Greek meaning of STEPHEN. St. STEPHEN is one of the seven men appointed by the Church at Jerusalem to aid the Apostles by ministering to the poor (Acts 6:1-6). From his Greek name, it seems that he may have been a Hellenistic Jew. St. STEPHEN was accused of blasphemy, and was stoned to death, thus, he became the first martyr for Christendom (Acts 7:57). The Orthodox Church observes the Feast of St. STEPHEN on December 27. Steve and Stevie are diminutives.
STEPHANIE (stef.'an.ē)	(F) Feminine form of STEPHEN. See STEPHEN. The Orthodox Church commemorates the memory of St. STEPHANIE on June 15.
STEROPE (ster.'oh.pē)	(F) From the Greek, the word means "lightning; twinkling." Sterope is one of the seven Pleiades.
STRATON (stra.'tohn)	(M) St. STRATON is the influential citizen who converted many to Christianity. He, successfully, discouraged people from attending immoral events, and was burned at the stake c. 301. The Orthodox Church commemorates his memory on August 17.
STYLIAN, STYLIANOS (stē.'lē.ahn), (stē.lē.an.'ohs)	(M) The feast of St. STYLIAN is celebrated in the Orthodox Church on November 26. Telly is a diminutive form.
STYLIANE (stē.lē.'an)	(F) Feminine form of STYLIAN. See STYLIAN.
SUSAN (sū.sahn')	(F) Variant spelling for Susanna. See SUSANNA.
SUSANNA (sū.san.'ah)	(F) In Hebrew, the name SUSANNA means "a lily." St. SUSANNA is the close friend of Mary Magdalene, who remained with the Apostles, shared in their work, assisted with serving the

also, Susannah the Deaconess—Dec. 15

145

"Communion Suppers," and administered to the sick (Luke 8:3). The Orthodox Church remembers St. SUSANNA on the Sunday of the Myrrh-Bearing Woman which is the second Sunday after Easter.

Sue, Suky, and Susie are diminutives.

SUSANNAH
(su.san.a)

(F) Variant forms of SUSANNA. See SUSANNA.

SUSETTE
(su.set)

(F) Variant forms of SUSANNA. See SUSANNA.

SYLVAN
(sil.vahn)

(M) Diminutive form of SILVANUS. See SILAS.

SYLVESTER
(sil.ves.tehr)

(M) Variant spelling of SILVESTER. See SILVESTER.

SYNTCHE
(sint.che)

(F) SYNTCHE, a female member of the Church at Philippi, is described by St. Paul as his fellow laborer (Philip 4:2-3). She is probably one of the first teachers of the early church, or she may have been a deaconess of the Church.

T

I would to God thou and I knew a commodity
of good names were to be bought.
--Shakespeare - **Henry IV**

TABITHA
(ta.bĩ'.thah)

(F) This Syrian word means "gazelle." TABITHA is the name of the pious Christian woman at Joppa, who believed in Christ, and was raised from the dead by St. Peter (Acts 9:36-43). See DORCAS. The feast of St. TABITHA is observed in the Orthodox Church on October 25.
Diminutive forms include Tabbie and Tabby.

TAKIS
(ta.kēs)

(M) Masculine diminutive form for Greek names such as Panagiotis - PANAGIOTAKIS, CHRISTOS, CHRISTAKIS.

TANIA, TANYA
(tan.'ē.ah), (tan.'yah)

(F) Russian form of TATIANA. See TATIANA.

TARASIOS
(ta.ras.'ē.uhs)

(M) St. TARASIOS, Patriarch of Constantinople, presided over the Council of Nicaea, which restored the veneration of icons in the Orthodox Church. He is remembered on February 25, in the Orthodox Church.
Terry is a diminutive form.

TASSO
(ta.'sō)

(M) Masculine diminutive form.

TATIANA
(ta.tē.an.'ah)

(F) "Silver-haired" is the Latin connotation of this name. St. TATIANA, the martyr, was put to death in Rome under Alexander Severus. She is remembered in the Orthodox Church on January 12.
Tatia and Anna are diminutive forms.

TATIANAS
(ta.tē.an.'ahs)

(F) Variant spellings of TATIANA. See TATIANA.

TATIANNAS
(ta.tē.ã.'nahs)

(F) Variant spellings of TATIANA. See TATIANA.

TATTA
(ta.'ta)

(F) St. TATTA, a Christian woman, is the wife of Paul and mother of Sebinian, Maximus, Rufus, and Eugene. They all died, under torture, in their native City of Damascus. The Orthodox Church observes the memory of St. TATTA on September 25.

TECLA, TECKLA
(tes.'lah), (tek.'lah)

(F) Variant spellings of THECKLA. See THECKLA.

TEGLA
(teg.'lah)

(F) Variant spelling of THECKLA. See THECKLA.

TELEMACHUS
(te.lem.'uh.kuhs)

(M) In ancient Greek mythology, TELEMACHUS is the son of Ulysseus and Penelope. In addition to the TELEMACHUS of mythology, a Christian TELEMACHUS is the Syrian monk who lived during the rule of Emperor Honorius (c. 400 A.D.). TELEMACHUS was so outraged with the gladiatorial events that he leaped into the arena at the Coliseum and attempted to separate the gladiators. In his endeavor, he lost his life at the hands of the rebellious crowd. His act made such an impression on Honorius that he discontinued the gladiatorial combats.

Telly is a diminutive form.

TERENCE
(ter.'ens)

(M) The name TERENCE is from a Roman gens. St. TERRENCE is a 3rd century saint, and the Orthodox Church observes his memory on October 28.

Terry is a diminutive form.

TERESA
(te.rē.'sah)

(F) A variant spelling of THERESA. See THERESA.

TERPSICHORE
(turp.sik.'uh.rē)

(F) TERPSICHORE is one of the Nine Muses of Greek mythology who was in charge of dancing and dramatic chorus.

Diminutives include Terpse, Terpsy, and Coré.

THADDEUS
(thad.ē.uhs)

(M) The Hebrew translation of this name is "breach." THADDEUS is the surname of the Apostle Jude (Mark 3:18), and his memory is observed on August 21, in the Orthodox Church.

Tad and Thad are diminutive forms of the name.

THAIS
(ta.ḗ)

(F) The name means "blooming" or "giving joy" in Greek. THAIS, a 4th century B.C. Greek hetaera, accompanied Alexander the Great on his expedition to Asia, and is said to have encouraged him to burn the palace of the Persian kings at Persepolis. In Church history of the 4th century, St. THAIS is the converted harlot. The Orthodox Church commemorates her memory on October 8.

The story of St. THAIS is told in a novel by Anatole France and in the opera by Jules Massenet.

THALIA
(tha.le.ah)

(F) THALIA, in Greek, means "blooming". The name THALIA appears twice in Greek mythology. THALIA is one of the Three Graces, and THALIA is one of the Nine Muses - the Muse of comedy and pastoral poetry.

THEA
(the.ah)

(F) THEA is translated, from the Greek, as "shinning." Christian women named THEA suffered a martyrs death, and the Orthodox Church observes their memory on February 23, June 25, and July 18.

THECKLA
(thek.lah)

(F) This name, from the Greek, means "divine fame." St. THECKLA is the renowned saint, of the 1st century, who is the first woman martyr. St. THECKIA was born of a noble family in Lycaonia, and was converted through the preaching of St. Paul. As a consequence, she suffered persecutions, both, from the family and the public. The Orthodox Church commemorates the memory of St. THECKLA the Great Martyr on September 24.

THEMIS
(the.mis)

(F) The name THEMIS, from the Greek, means "order and justice." THEMIS, of Greek mythology, is the daughter of Uranus and Gaea, and she and Zeus preside over law and order. THEMIS is pictured as the blindfolded goddess with scales in one hand and a cornucopia in the other hand.

THEMISTOCLES
(theh.mis.tuh.klez)

(M) The name THEMISTOCLES, which means "to the glory of Themis," brings to mind that ancient Greek general and statesman, who was, undoubtedly, the savior of Athens and Greece during the crisis at Salamis. The name appears, again, in the annals of Church history as St. THEMISTOCLES, the martyr. THEMISTOCLES is a shepherd of Myra, who was beheaded for refusing to reveal the hiding place of a fellow Christian. The Orthodox Church honors his memory on December 21.

Themis and Takis are diminutive forms.

THEOCHARIS
(theh.ō.kar.'uhs)

(M) Variant spelling of THEOHARIS. See THEOHARIS.

THEODORA
(theh.ō.dor.'ah)

(F) The combination of the two Greek words "theos = god" and doro = gift" gives meaning to THEODORA as "gift of God." Many Christian women named THEODORA achieved sainthood, and are remembered in the Orthodox Church on September 11, November 15, March 11, 20 and April 2, 5, and 16. In addition to these pious women, St. THEODORA the Empress is honored on February 11. It was she, who fought, valiantly, to restore the icons in the Orthodox Church. Through her efforts in 834 A.D., the General Council convened and formally accepted the veneration again of icons in the Orthodox Church.
Dora and Theo are diminutive forms.

THEODORE
(thē.ō.dor)

(M) Masculine form of THEODORA. See THEODORA. The list of men named THEODORE, who gave their lives for Christ, is long and noble. Some of the dates which are observed in their memory are November 24, 28, February 8, 17, March 6, and May 8, and 25. On the first Saturday of Lent, the Orthodox Church observes the heroic martyrdom of St. THEODORE, who dies for Christ rather than renounce Him.
Diminutives include Ted and Teddy.

THEODOSIA
(thē.uh.dō.'shah)

(F) Feminine of THEODOSIOS. See THEODOSIOS. St. THEODOSIA is the mother of St. Procopius, and she suffered a martyr's death at Caesarea in Palestine under Diocletion. The Orthodox Church observes May 29, in her memory.

THEOGENES
(thē.'uh.juh.nēz)

(M) This name, THEOGENES, is from the Greek and means "divine birth." In ancient Greek history, THEOGENES is a member of The Thirty at Athens. A Christian THEOGENES gave his life for Christ, and the Orthodox Church solemnizes the memory of St. THEOGENES on January 2.
Gene and Theo are diminutive forms.

THEOHARIS
(thē.uh.har.'uhs)

(M) "Divine grace" is the meaning of this Greek name. The feast day for St. Theoharis is observed by the Orthodox Church on Wednesday of Easter Week.
Diminutive forms are Theo and Haris.

THEOLA
(thē.ō.'lah)

(F) "Heavenly sent" is the translation of this Greek name.

THEONA,
THEONAS
(theh.ō.′nah),
(thā.ō.′nahs)

(F) This name means "godly" in Greek. The Orthodox Church observes the memory of St. THEONA on January 5, April 4, and 24.

THEOPHANE
(theh.of.′an.ē)

(M/F) THEOPHANE is from the Greek words "theo = god; phainen = to show" which means "the manifestation of God to man." The feast of Epiphany, on January 6, is the date when those who have this name generally, observe the feast day. Furthermore, the Orthodox Church commemorates the memory of those pious people named THEOPHANE, who gave their life for Christ, on September 9, October 11, December 16, March 12, May 10, June 8, and 10. See TIFFANY.

THEOPHILIA
(theh.ō.fil.′ē.ah)

(F) Feminine of THEOPHILOS. See THEOPHILOS.
Diminutives include Philia and Theo.

THEOPHILOS
(theh.of.′uh.los)

(M) "Friend of God" is the literal meaning of this Greek name. THEOPHILOS is the one whom St. Luke addressed in both his Gospel and Acts as "the most excellent Theophilos" (Luke 1:3; Acts 1:1). He, perhaps, was a convert through Paul's teachings at Rome, and the title "most excellent" suggests he was a high official. The Orthodox Church commemorates his memory on July 21.
Phil, Philo, and Theo are diminutive forms.

THERA
(thē.′rah)

(F) The Greek meaning of THERA is "untamed."

THERESA
(tah.rē.′sah)

(F) The name THERESA means "the harvester" in Greek. Feminine form of THERESOS. See THERESOS.
Terry is a diminutive form.

THERESOS
(tah.rē.′sohs)

(M) St. THERESOS, bishop, is remembered in the Orthodox Church on August 5.
Terry is a diminutive form.

THETIS
(thē.′tis)

(F) THETIS, in Greek mythology, is the beautiful nymph of the sea.

THOMAIS
(tō.′ma.ēs)

(F) Feminine of THOMAS. See THOMAS. St. THOMAIS, the Alexandrian woman and wife of a fisherman, is tempted to commit an immoral act by her father-in-law. When THOMAIS refused, he murdered her. The Orthodox Church observes her memory on April 14.

THOMAS (tom.´ahs)	(M) THOMAS, in Hebrew, means "a twin." St. THOMAS is the Apostle who doubted our Lord's Resurrection (John 20:19-29). Holy Tradition relates that St. THOMAS preached in India, and was martyred on Mount Saint THOMAS near Madras. The Orthodox Church commemorates the memory of St. THOMAS on October 6, and on the first Sunday after Easter. Tom and Tommy are diminutives of the name.
THOMASA (tom.´ah.sa)	(F) Feminine form of THOMAS.
THOMASINA (tom.ah.se.´nah)	(F) Feminine form of THOMAS.
TIFFANY (tif.´ah.ne)	(F) See THEOPHANE. TIFFANY is the English corruption of THEOPHANY.
TIMON (ti.´mohn)	(M) "Honoring" is the meaning of this Greek name. St. TIMON is one of the seven original Deacons at Jerusalem (Acts 6:5), and is memorialized by the Orthodox Church on July 28.
TIMOTHEA (tim.uh.the.´ah)	(F) Feminine of TIMOTHY. See TIMOTHY.
TIMOTHY (tim.uh.the)	(M) "Honoring God" is the translation of this name from the Greek. There are many saints named TIMOTHY whom the Orthodox Church honors throughout the year. Some dates are November 5, 10, 28, December 19, January 22, February 27, June 10, and August 1, and 16. The celebrated TIMOTHY is the helper of St. Paul. TIMOTHY received instructions and prayers from his grandmother Lois and from his mother Eunice, and this, coupled, with the preaching of St. Paul, led to his conversion. TIMOTHY became a disciple and companion of Paul, and Paul mentions him often in his Epistles, especially, in the New Testament book, Epistle to Timothy. The Orthodox Church observes his memory on January 22. Tim is a diminutive form.
TINA (te.´nah)	(F) A Greek diminutive form for Constantina, Christina.
TINO (te.´no)	(M) A Greek diminutive form for Constantine.
TITO (te.´to)	(M) A variant form of TITUS. See TITUS.

TITUS (tī.tuhs)	(M) The name is from the Greek and means "honored." St. TITUS is the distinguished Christian minister of Greek origin, who was converted under the preaching of St. PAUL (Galatians 2:3). He became a helper of Paul, and it was to TITUS that Paul wrote the Epistle to TITUS. TITUS became the first bishop of Crete, where he died. The Orthodox Church commemorates the feast of St. TITUS on August 25.
TOBIAH (tō.bī.ah) **TOBIAS** (tō.bī.ahs)	(M) This name is from the Hebrew and is translated as "God is good." St. TOBIAS is venerated in the Orthodox Church on November 2. Toby is a diminutive form.
TOMAS (tō.mahs)	(M) A variant spelling of THOMAS. See THOMAS.
TOULA (tōō.lah)	(F) A Greek diminutive for names such as Spyridoula.
TRIFON, **TRIFONOS** (trī.fuhn), (trī.fuh.nuhs)	(M) St. TRIFON, martyr, is honored in the Orthodox Church on February 1.
TRYPHENA (trī.fē.nah)	(F) St. TRYPHENA is one of the early workers in the Church at Rome. St. Paul sent greetings to her because she had served the Church so faithfully (Romans 16:12). The Orthodox Church commemorates the memory of St. TRYPHENA on January 31, and April 11. Terry and Fena are diminutives of the name.
TRYPHON (trī.fuhn)	(M) Variant spelling of TRIFON. See TRIFON.
TYCHON (tik.ohn)	(M) In Greek mythology, TYCHON is the goddess of Fortune. A Christian man named TYCHON became bishop in Cyprus and is remembered on June 16. St. TYCHON energetically fought against the last remnants of paganism in the island of Cyprus.

U

My name is Might-have-been;
I am also called No-more, Too-late
Farewell.
--Dante Gabriel Rosseti

ULYSSES
(ū.lis.'sehs)

(M) ULYSSES is the Latin equivalent of ODYSSEUS and means "a hater." ULYSSES is the legendary king of Ithaca, one of the leading chieftains in Homer's **Iliad.** He is the hero of **The Odyssey,** and is noted for being wise, eloquent, and ingenious.

URANIA
(ū.rā.'nē.ah)

(F) URANIA in Greek means "the heavenly one," and URANIA is one of the Nine Muses of Greek mythology - the Muse of Astrology. The English equivalent is CELESTE. See CELESTE.

URBAN
(ur.'bahn)

(M) This name, from the Latin, means "from the city". URBAN appears in Romans 16:9, and he is the Roman disciple and Paul's companion in Christian labors. URBAN was ordained a bishop by St. Andrew, and became Bishop of all Macedonia. He was martyred in his service of the Lord, and the Orthodox Church commemorates his memory on October 3.

URIEL
(ū.'ri.el)

(M) URIEL is one of the seven archangels sent by God to answer the questions of Esdras. (II Esdras 4).

V

VALENCIA
(va.len.'shah)

(F) Variant form of VALENTINA.

VALENTE
(va.len.'tē)

(F) Variant form of VALENTINA.

VALENTIA
(va.len.'te.ah)

(F) Feminine of VALENTINE. See VALENTINE. Val and Valtie are diminutive forms.

VALENTINA
(va.len.tē.'nah)

(F) Feminine of VALENTINE. See VALENTINE. Val and Valtie are diminutive forms.

VALENTINE
(va.leń.tin)

(M) "Healthy, strong" is the meaning of this Latin name. St. VALENTINE is the priest in Rome (c. 270 A.D.), who was imprisoned for giving aid to persecuted Christians, and was, finally, clubbed to death. The Orthodox Church commemorates his memory on April 24.

VALERIA,
(va.ler.ē.ah)
VALERIE
(val.'uh.rē)

(F) Feminine of VALERIAN. See VALERIAN. The Orthodox Church commemorates the memory of St. VALERIA on June 8.

VALERIAN
(va.ler.'ē.ahn)

(M) VALERIAN is a famous Latin gens, and has its roots in Latin meaning "belonging to VALENTINE." St. VALERIAN, the martyr, is honored in the Orthodox Church on November 22.

VALIANT
(val.'yuhnt)

(M) A variant form of VALENTINE. See VALENTINE.

VANESSA
(van.es.'ah)

(F) This Greek word means "butterfly." The diminutives are Van and Vannie.

VARVARA
(var.́var.ah)

(F) A variant spelling of BARBARA. See BARBARA.

VASILI
(va.sē.́lē)

(M) A variant spelling of BASIL. See BASIL.

VASILIKE
(va.sē.lē.ke)́

(F) Variant spelling of BASILIKE. See BASILIKE.

VASILIKI
(va.sē.lē.ke)́

(F) Variant spelling of BASILIKE. See BASILIKE.

VERA
(ver.́ah)

(F) VERA is from Latin and is translated as "true," but it is more directly from the Russian and means "faith." It is, also, a diminutive form of VERONICA. See VERONICA.

VERONICA
(ver.on.́uh.ka)

(F) The name VERONICA, possibly, is translated from the Latin and is translated as "true image;" however, it is possible that the name is derived from BERENICE. See BERENICE.

According to Holy Tradition, a woman of Jerusalem handed her headcloth to Jesus on His way to Calvary, and He wiped His brow and returned it to her. The headcloth was found to bear the perfect likeness upon it. It was called "Vera = true, Icon = likeness." The woman of Jerusalem became St. VERONICA. The Orthodox Church reveres the memory of St. VERONICA, holy martyr, on July 12.

VICTOR
(vik.́tuhr)

(M) In Latin, this name means "a conqueror." Several men named VICTOR died for Christ, and the Orthodox Church observes their memory on November 11, February 26, April 20, July 6, and August 20. The name VICTOR is an equivalent for the Greek name NIKETAS.

VICTORIA
(vik.tor.́ē.ah)

(F) Feminine form of VICTOR. See VICTOR. VICTORIA is the English equivalent of the Greek name Nike.

VICTORIE
(vik.́tor.ē)

(F) Variant spelling for VICTORIA. See VICTORIA.

VICTORINE
(vik.́tuh.rēn)

(F) Variant spelling for VICTORIA. See VICTORIA.

VIDA
(vī.́dah)

(F) Feminine diminutive form of DAVID. See DAVID.

VINCENT
(vin.́suhnt)

(M) "The conqueror; victorious" is the Latin connotation of this name. The Orthodox Church observes the following date for the martyrs named VINCENT: November 11, December 11, and January 22.

Vin and Vince are diminutive forms.

VINCENTIA
(vin.sen.́shah)

(F) Feminine of VINCENT. See VINCENT.

VIOLA
(vī.ō.́lah)

(F) A variant form of VIOLET. See VIOLET.

VIOLET
(vī.uh.let)

(F) VIOLET is from the Latin and means "modest; shy."

VIOLETTA
(vē.uh.let.́ah)

(F) Variant form of VIOLET. See VIOLET.

VIOLETTE
(vē.uh.let)́

(F) Variant form of VIOLET. See VIOLET.

VIRGINIA
(vir.jin.́ē.ah)

(F) "Virgin, pure" is the Latin translation of this name. Ginger, Ginny, Jimmy, Virg, and Virgy are among the diminutive forms of the name.

VIRGINIE
(vir.jin.́ē)

(F) Variant spelling of VIRGINIA. See VIRGINIA.

VITALIS
(vī.ta.́luhs)

(M) The Orthodox Church commemorates the memory of St. VITALIS, a saint of the 3rd century, on January 11.

VIVIAN
(vi.vē.́uhn)

(F) Feminine of VIVIEN. See VIVIEN. The feast of St. VIVIAN, a virgin martyr, is commemorated on March 9, in the Orthodox Church.

Vi, Viv, Vivi, Vivia and Vivie are among the diminutives.

VIVIANE
(vi.vē.́an)

(F) Variant spelling of VIVIAN. See VIVIAN.

VIVIENNE
(vi.vī.́en)

(F) Variant spelling of VIVIAN. See VIVIAN.

VIVIEN
(vi.vē.́ehn)

(M) "Lively, full of life" is the Latin meaning of this name. The Orthodox Church commemorates the memory of St. VIVIEN on March 9.

VLADAMER,
VLADIMER
(vla.́dah.mer)
(vla.́dah.mehr)

(M) In the Slavic languages, VLADIMER means "the ruler of all." St. VLADIMER is the Prince of Kiev, and venerated apostle of Russia (1015). VLADIMER was baptized before his marriage to the sister of the Byzantine emperor. He invited the Greek clergy to evangelize Russia. His memory is observed on May 22, in the Orthodox Church.

VOULA
(vōṓ.lah)

(F) A Greek diminutive form for names such as Paraskeve - Paraskevoula, See - oula.

X

There stands a shadow - of a glorious name.   --Lucan

XANTHE
(zan.ʹthē)

(F) XANTHE means "blonde" in Greek. St. XANTHE, the martyr is memorialized on March 9, in the Orthodox Church.

XANTHIPPE
(zan.tip.ʹē)

(F) "A light colored horse" is the meaning of this Greek name. In ancient Greek history, XANTHIPPE is the wife of the philosopher Socrates. A Christian XANTHIPPE named, the Righteous, is remembered on September 23, in the Orthodox Church.

XENA
(zē.ʹnah)
XENIA
(zen.ʹē.ah)

(F) This Greek name means "hospitable." St. XENA the Righteous is memorialized on January 24, in the Orthodox Church.

XIMENA
(zē.mē.ʹnah)

(F) "Heroine" is the Greek meaning of this name.

Y

YANNIS
(yan.´ihs)

(M) Greek diminutive form for JOHN. See JOHN.

YASMIN
(yas.´min)

(F) Arabic form of JASMIN. See JASMIN.

YURI
(yū.re´)

(M) Russian form of GEORGE. See GEORGE.

YUSUF
(yū.´suhf)

(M) Arabic form of JOSEPH. See JOSEPH.

Z

"I have hallowed this house, which thou has built to put my name there forever; and mine eyes and mine heart shall be there perpetually."
I Kings 9:3

ZACCHEUS
(za.kā.uhs)

(M) In Hebrew, this name means "innocent, pure." ZACCHEUS is the Greek form of the Hebrew ZACCAI (Luke 19:1-10). ZACCHEUS is the wealthy Jew of Jericho, who climbed a sycamore tree so that he could see Jesus as He passed by. The Orthodox Church observes the memory of ZACCHEUS on April 20.

Zach is a diminutive form of the name.

ZACHARIAH
(zek.ah.rī.ah)

(M) "Remembered by the Lord" is the translation of this name from the Hebrew. ZACHARIAH is the Old Testament martyr who was slain in the temple between the Altar and the Holy Place (Luke 11:51). His memory is commemorated on September 5. ZACHARIAH is the father of St. John the Baptist (Luke 1), and the Orthodox Church commemorates his memory on September 5, also.

Zach and Zack are diminutive forms.

ZACHARIAS
(zak.ah.rī.uhs)

(M) Variant spelling of ZACHARIAH. See ZACHARIAH.

ZACHARY
(zak.ah.rē)

(M) Variant spellings of ZACHARIAH. See ZACHARIAH.

ZEKE
(zēk)

(M) A diminutive form of EZEKIEL. See EZEKIEL.

ZENA
(zē.nah)

(F) Name is a form of XENA and means "a gift of ZEUS" in Greek. St. ZENA, martyr, is remembered on October 11, in the Orthodox Church.

ZENNAS
(zē.nas)

(M) A variant spelling of ZENOS. See ZENOS.

ZENOBIA
(zen.o.be.ah)

(F) The Greek meaning of this name is "having life from Zeus". October 30, is observed in memory of St. ZENOBIA, martyr, in the Orthodox Church.

ZENOS
(ze.nohs)

(M) "Zeus' gift" is the translation of this Greek name. St. ZENOS is of African origin, and he was a hard working priest. St. ZENOS built churches and founded a convent for virgins before St. Ambrose founded his monastery. St. ZENOS died in 371 A.D., and the Orthodox Church observes his feast day on February 10.

ZEPHANIAH
(zef.ah.ni.ah)

A Hebrew prophet of seventh century B.C.

ZOA, ZOIE
(zo.a), (zo.e)

(F) Variant spellings of ZOE. See ZOE.

ZOE
(zo.e)

(F) ZOE means "life" in Greek. ZOE, Exuperius (Hesperius), Cyriacus, and Theodulus were a family of slaves - wife, husband and two sons -who were owned by a rich pagan in Pamphylia. They refused to take part, with their master, in idolatrous rites and were martyred. The Orthodox Church observes May 2, in honor of St. ZOE.

ZOSIMA
(zo.sim.ah)

(F) "Woman of wealth" is the connotation of this Greek name. St. Zosima is remembered in the Orthodox Church on January 24, and April 4.

ZOSIMOS
(zo.sim.ohs)

(M) Masculine of ZOSIMA. See ZOSIMA. The Orthodox Church commemorates the memory of St. ZOSIMOS, martyr, on January 4.

ZOTICOS
(zo.tuh.kuhs)

(M) St. Zoticos is the protector of orphans, and the Orthodox Church commemorates his memory on December 31.

BIBLIOGRAPHY

Anderson, Christopher, P., **The Name Game,** New York: Simon and Schuster, 1977.

Book of Saints. Benedictine Monks of St. Augustine Abbey (4th ed.) New York: The Macmillan Co., 1947.

Brewer's Dictionary of Phrase and Fable, Ivory H. Evans Ed. New York: Harper and Row, 1981.

Callinikos, C. **History of the Orthodox Church.** Los Angelos, California: Prothymus Press, 1957.

Deen, Edity. **All the Women of the Bible,** New York: Harper and Brothers, 1955.

Dictionary of the Holy Bible, New York: American Tract Society, 1878.

Farmer, David. **Oxford Dictionary of Saints,** Oxford: Oxford University Press, 1978.

Gegle, G.S. **Menaion,** Athens, Greece: M.I. Salisberous, 1904.

The Greek New Testament, Stuttgart, West Germany: Wurttemburg Bible Society, 1966.

Hamilton, Edith, **Mythology.** New York: American Library, 1942.

Iliad of Homer. Louise R. Loomis, Ed. New York: Walter J. Black, Inc. 1942.

Kalberer, Augustine. **Lives of the Saints.** Chicago: Franciscan Herald Press, 1975.

Lambert, Eloise, Pei, Mario. **Our Names: Where they came from and What they mean.** New York: Lothrop, Lee and Shephard Co., 1969.

A Lexican Abridged from Liddell and Scott Greek - English Lexicon. J.M. Whitan, ed., New York: Harper and Brothers, 1887.

McBirnie, W.S. **The Search for the Twelve Apostles,** Wheaton, Ill.: Tyndale Publishing, Inc., 1973.

Nassar, S. **Book of Divine Prayer and Services,** New York: Blackhaw Press, 1938.

New International Version of the Holy Bible, Grand Rapids, Michigan: Zondervan Bible Publishers. 1978.

Nicozisin, George. **A History of the Church,** Parts II and III, Greek Orthodox Archdiocese of N. and S. America, 1972.

Poulos, George. **Lives of the Saints and Major Feast Days,** Boston: Greek Orthodox Archdiocese of N. and S. American, 1974.

_____**Orthodox Saints,** Brookline, Mass: Holy Cross Orthodox Press, 1976.

Sleigh, Lo and Johnson, C. **The Book of Girls' Names,** New York Thomas Cromwell Co., 1962.

Stewart, George R. **American Given Names,** New York: Oxford University Press, 1979.

Wolverton, R.E. **An Outline of Classical Mythology,** Totowa, N.J.: Littlefield Quality Paperbacks, 1971.

Zimmerman, J.B. **Dicitionary of Classical Mythology,** New York: Bantam Books, 1964.